The Weather Changers

Other books by D. S. Halacy, Jr.

The Coming Age of Solar Energy
Computers: The Machines We Think With
Cyborg: Evolution of the Superman

The
Weather
Changers

D. S. Halacy, Jr.

HARPER & ROW, PUBLISHERS

New York, Evanston, and London

Contents

Foreword

THIS is a good book. It has something for everybody, whether experienced professional or merely interested layman.

The author starts out by clarifying the authorship of the now hackneyed, "Everybody talks about the weather, but nobody does anything about it." As a source of extremely interesting and often as surprising information as the authorship of the famous quote, the book keeps its promise. As a compendium of interesting facts and history and a glimpse into the future, I recommend it heartily to all, young and old.

However, a word of caution: Although the book has something for everyone and will not bore the mature scientist, it cannot be everything for everyone. It is not, and does not claim to be, an elementary or advanced textbook. The author does not try to explain meteorological phenomena. It would take a fairly long shelf of books to advance even modestly sophisticated explanations of the extremely broad spectrum of topics that are covered. He relies very heavily on the average "intuition" in predicting weather phenomena, and most "explanations" are quite superficial. This does not weaken the book at all, because there is a wealth of text material for the person who wishes to go into the subjects more deeply. In fact, the avoidance of attempts to give even elementary explanations is sensible and keeps the book readable—and readable it is.

Few people appreciate the complexity of the field of weather modification. Intentionally or otherwise, man is modifying his environment. Two decades have passed since Langmuir's dramatic pioneering attempts at cloud seeding. The first was a period of great optimism. The second was characterized by much reservation. Once again we see the emergence of optimism, tempered, now, with some caution because we know more about the complications in meteorological processes than we did twenty years ago when things seemed simpler in the cloud than they do now. But even as we realize the difficulties in dealing with simple cloud systems, we are becoming increasingly aware of how, through air pollution, for example, man has created problems for himself in modifying the weather that make the difficulties to be encountered in natural processes seem quite tame.

Author Halacy makes quite a good general statement on the elements of weather and attempts at forecasting—with a very pleasant balance between the humorous and the profound. This balance is maintained with a very scholarly chapter on the history of rainmaking, in which even the most advanced researcher will find material he probably has not contacted before.

The various aspects of modern weather modification are, then, presented in good perspective, not only as far as rainmaking is concerned, but also with respect to hail suppression, fog dissipation, lightning suppression, and hurricane modification. After an excursion into the general topic of inadvertent weather modification due to urbanization and the works of men, there is an excellent summary of the history of legal action and the legal problems to expect in the future, internationally and regionally.

It is quite clear that this whole topic is going to have a continually increasing impact on our lives, intentionally or accidentally. People are going to have to make important judgments via their legislatures or otherwise. It is quite imperative that people become better informed in this whole area. The pressures of population increase make it clear that we will live with increasing controls. Controls on the weather, either via prevention of fouling our atmospheres or via regulating our climates for population accommodation, are inevitable. No other book that I know of gives as comprehensive a picture as does this one. That it can be read with ease and pleasure is a very lucky thing, and I recommend it to you highly.

Dr. A. Richard Kassander, Director
Institute of Atmospheric Physics, The University of Arizona

The Rhyme of the Rain Machine

Said Jeremy Jonathan Joseph Jones,
"The weather is far too dry.
So I reckon I'll have to stir my bones
And try the effect of the concussive tones
Upon the lazy sky."

So Jeremy Jonathan Joseph went
Away to the nearest town
And there his money was quickly spent
For queer contraptions all intent
To make the rain come down.

There were cannon, and mortars, and lots of shells
And dynamite by the ton
With a gas balloon and a chime of bells
And various other mystic spells
To overcloud the sun.

The day was fair and the sky was bright
And never a cloud was seen
When Jeremy Jonathan set alight
His biggest fuse and screwed up tight
The joints of the rain machine.

He fired a shot and barely two
When the sky began to pale
The third one brought a heavy dew
But at the fourth tornadoes blew
With thunder, rain and hail.

It rained all night and another day
And then for a week or more
It flooded the farm in a scandalous way
And drowned poor Jeremy, sad to say,
Who couldn't stop the pour.

Oh, Jeremy Jonathan Joseph Jones,
Your farm was fair to see
But now a lake lies over its stones
From whose dark bosom horrific moans
Are heard nocturnallee.

To check the flood you started, I've heard,
All efforts were in vain
Until the Bureau at Washington stirred
And stopped the storm with a single word,
By just predicting—Rain!

—F. W. CLARKE
Life, November 5, 1891

"Everybody talks about the weather but nobody does anything about it."

—Statement claimed by Charles Dudley Warner but
generally attributed to SAMUEL LANGHORNE CLEMENS

1

The Weather Changers

ONE of the most challenging prospects for scientists and
engineers in this age of nuclear power, space exploration, and
biological advances has to do with the most mundane subject
in the world—the weather. In sight is control of even the long-
range weather we call climate. The late John von Neumann,
the scientific genius who did so much for the electronic computer, said that it might be easier to control weather than to
predict it. He was not being facetious. Weather prediction has
been found to be fantastically difficult; but the high-speed computer seems to be moving us perceptibly toward the goal of
accurate prediction. And with more success in forecasting the
weather, man is learning how to change it too.

Because a global water crisis exists, there is powerful moti-
vation for weather modification to produce more rain, or to
redistribute the amount that now falls. Secretary of the Interior
Stewart Udall, embroiled in a bitter water battle with his own
state of Arizona, predicts that the chorus Americans soon will be
singing is "How dry I am!"

In 1965 the United States government spent $11½ billion on
space programs, $212 million on land, $72 million on oceanog-
raphy, $94 million on atmospheric sciences, but only a minuscule

1

$4 million on actual weather-modification work. President Lyndon B. Johnson in that year pointed out that the "rivers in the sky" represented a rich source of additional water flowing overhead, and called for increased effort to tap that source.

The scientific and engineering obstacles that must be overcome rank in magnitude with those encountered in developing peaceful uses of nuclear power and compare with those now being encountered in our attempts to place a man on the moon. Substantial progress has been made, but the pace has been slow. To advance the rate of progress, an effort of larger scope and direction is needed both in conducting basic research and in developing means to put the knowledge to work.

The first legislation concerned with rainmaking was Public Law 79-691, passed in 1946, soon after Vincent Schaefer's dry-ice experiments. Interest in formal government research into practical weather modification began several years later with Senate Bill 5, introduced in the 82nd Congress. This legislation provided for research to produce more water from salt-water sources or the atmosphere. Out of it came an amended bill, Senate Bill 2225, calling for a weather-modification program. This bill resulted in Public Law 83-256, creating the Advisory Committee on Weather Control in 1953. Public Law 84-664 in 1956 extended the Advisory Committee until 1958, at which time Public Law 85-510 directed the National Science Foundation to initiate and support a program of study, research, and evaluation in the field of weather modification.

The Bureau of Reclamation of the Department of the Interior was granted an appropriation of about $1 million in 1965 and about $3 million in 1966 for research toward supplementing the water available in the Colorado River Basin by weather modification.

Currently under study are two bills, S.2916 and S.2875. The first would transfer authority for weather modification from the National Science Foundation to the Environmental Science Services Administration of the Department of Commerce. The second would assign responsibility to the Department of the Interior. S.2875 provides for appropriations of $35 million in the first year, $50 million in the second, and $70 million in the third.

The battle for weather modification has been as stormy as the weather it deals with. Charges and countercharges involve such items as "a lost decade" in rainmaking, the amount of money spent in a recent year on modification research (with figures ranging from $4 million to more than $400 million!), and the number of agencies participating. The controversy has ranged a group of influential legislators against distinguished atmospheric scientists, rainmaking partisans against Federal agencies, and some of those agencies against one another. One writer termed a voluminous National Academy of Science panel report "a big wet blanket." The Senate has been called "wishy-washy" by some, yet hailed by others as interested in producing water while a "Cosmos Club crowd" of scientists prefers an output of papers. For every claim of breakthrough, there are accusations of "breakdown" instead. With all the heat produced, however, there has also been light and even some precipitation. Although only a token sum was expended in 1966, weather modification and control seems to have come of age, and in scientific interest ranks only slightly below space, computers, and nuclear energy. In 1966 two definitive reports were published, one by the National Academy of Sciences and the other by the National Science Foundation. The major problem seems to be which branch or branches of government shall be responsible for the programs sure to come.

Despite the fact that the new science and technology is such a glamour baby, it still remains one of the smallest with regard to Federal support for the research projects involved. Authorities point to two reasons for this lag in effort. First, no formal national goal has been set for weather modification and control, as has been done with nuclear energy and the space race. And although the potential benefits of weather changing are obviously tremendous, the machinery of implementing it is not as straightforward as that of computers, which are enjoying a great boom and profiting their manufacturers as well as the user. Second, the field of weather modification itself is a vague, hard-to-define area. Seeding a cloud and making rain is a dramatic demonstration, but this is only a small part of the business of weather modification. Much of the required effort lies in research into the nature of weather and also into the improvement of prediction techniques. These endeavors lack the popular appeal that actual rainmaking itself has always had; the weatherman has long been with us and is not an especially exciting person. The National Academy of Sciences report defines weather modification this way:

The subject of weather and climate modification is concerned with any artificially produced changes in the composition, behavior, or dynamics of the atmosphere. Such changes may or may not be predictable, their production may be deliberate or inadvertent, they may be transient or permanent, and they may be manifested on any scale from the microclimate of plants to the macrodynamics of the worldwide atmospheric circulation.

The immediate interest of the Federal agencies active in weather modification is the application of existing technology to meet some aspect of recognized social need. Such needs may include national defense, health of the people, and maintenance of water resources. Other goals include development of new technology, basic and applied research, plus regulatory activities necessary to ensure that the public interest is served.

Federal support of weather modification in 1966 jumped to about $7 million, with eight Federal agencies participating: the departments of Agriculture, Commerce, Army, Navy, Air Force, and Interior, NASA (National Aeronautics and Space Administration), and the National Science Foundation. The Federal Aviation Agency has also been asked to plan a fog-dissipation program for United States airports.

In 1965, the most recent year for which full figures are available, there were a total of seventy-nine weather-modification field operations reported. These took place in twenty-five of the United States and several countries in the Western Hemisphere. Rainmaking was most popular, with sixty operations devoted to increasing precipitation. The others included fog dispersal, reduction of hail, and miscellaneous testing purposes.

Rainmakers are actively engaged in increasing the precipitation from the rivers in the sky. Dozens of commercial firms are seeding the clouds under contract to farmers and others; one firm does a million dollars in business a year. For power companies the rainmakers increase the snowpack above dams; city fathers pay for additional acre-feet of water in reservoirs. Ranchers concerned over wheat and other crops pay for hail abatement,

U.S. Air Force

Eleven pounds of dry ice dropped by Air Force scientists punched this three-mile hole in the clouds.

and airports sponsor fog-dispersal flights that permit thousands of passengers to complete their trips.

While some scientists protest that there is not yet, and will not be for a long time, the statistical proof of the effectiveness of cloud seeding, rainmakers point to empirical results: Their clients get more precipitation or less hail than do unseeded surrounding areas. Russia, with a weather-modification effort estimated at the equivalent of $20 million yearly, claims to have increased rainfall appreciably, and to have significantly reduced hail damage.

There are more exotic methods of weather changing, such as seeding the thunderclouds with "chaff," the strips of metal foil familiar to electronic-countermeasures experts of World War II and later, and electrifying the air beneath clouds with miles of steel wire to alter the nature of electrical storms.

The modern era of weather changing began one winter day in New York state when Vincent Schaefer of General Electric seeded a cloud with a few pounds of dry ice and caused snow to fall. Within a few years Irving Langmuir, General Electric scientist and Nobel Prize winner, claimed he had caused a hurricane to swerve, and significantly changed the pattern of rainfall in the United States—using a little dry ice in the first instance and some silver iodide smoke in the second.

The real beginning of weather modification took place in prehistoric times. Man being the dissatisfied creature he is, the notion of changing the weather must have come to him early. It is suggested not too facetiously that as soon as he could think he thought about changing things. One of the tasks of early magicians—and one that clings today—was the creation of rain by a variety of methods from the smearing of witch doctors with blood and chicken feathers (to resemble clouds!) to burning sacrificial fires and staging rain dances. Early men of religion also dealt in weather control; the concept of praying for rain indicates man's belief that the natural course of meteorological events can be altered by propitiation.

Behind this desire to tamper with nature's workings was usually a good reason. Droughts, military engagements, heat—all benefit from the onset of bountiful rains. And with a surfeit of moisture, man prayed for dry weather. Today there are many occasions when it seems we could better our lot by recourse to pushbutton weather. Over and above the desirability of good weather for Easter Sunday, parades, and sports events, the water crisis in many parts of the world indicates a need for more water than the skies normally provide in some places. As population overflows the regions naturally favored for habitation, it would be wonderful if we could make the deserts "bloom as the rose" and the frozen north melt to springlike warmth. We need water for itself, and for the blessing it brings indirectly.

Another reason for weather control is the elimination of death tolls and heavy property damage caused by hurricanes and tornadoes as well as by winter's ice and snowstorms. Lightning is destructive to life and property, and if we could learn to pull these fangs of the thunderstorm it would be worth our while. Forest fires threaten our civilization periodically, and the ability to produce rain over flaming wooded areas is highly desirable. Rainmakers in Canada and Australia have already conjured up just such a natural aerial water brigade!

New Tools

Men dreamed of unleashing the power of the atom long before 1945; then suddenly it was a dream no more, but an accomplished fact with far more potential than imagined. To some degree, this is also true of weather modification as art or science. Interestingly, nuclear explosives are at once accused of accidentally altering the weather and hailed as a means of taming it as well. There are other tools, including the computer, already mentioned, and weather satellites. The total adds up to new hope for proponents of man-made weather and climate.

The greatest advance, however, is that of *scientific* artificial rainmaking. For centuries many men have claimed rainmaking ability, and even "caused" torrential rains that flooded the countryside. Only in the mid-1940's did scientific cloud seeding arrive, however, although it must be admitted that the techniques of some of the old rainmakers were remarkably like the new idea of providing freezing nuclei for raindrops.

Irving Langmuir seeded clouds in New Mexico for weeks, and was satisfied that he had caused a pattern of rain that prevailed on the east coast. Lesser neo-rainmakers took up cloud seeding, and commercial operations began, to become a million-dollar business fraught with lawsuits over rain that fell and also that which did not.

Fog has plagued mankind, particularly in London, for centuries. In World War II man did something about these low clouds. A fog-dispersal system called FIDO (Fog, Investigations Dispersal Of) proved that the application of sufficient heat to the air could burn away fog and thus permit aircraft to land. Today many other methods clear the air of fog.

Airplanes flying over Italy are on the alert for irate farmers firing rockets high into the sky. The farmers aren't angry at the planes, but aim at harmful hailstones manufactured by thunderclouds. According to the rocket proponents, this technique softens the hailstones to the consistency of mush so they cause less damage when they strike crops.

For as long as some men have been trying to alter the weather, others have been accused of doing just that by accident, incident, or plain inadvertence. Cutting down the forests of Europe and America, cried many, caused the rains to go away. Stripping the top from grasslands caused the Dust Bowl droughts—and dry begot dry, just as rain begot rain. War was accused of causing rain, because of its cannon shot. Later on, radio was charged with upsetting the atmosphere and causing droughts. The atom bomb, when it came, suffered a like condemnation. These last charges may be well founded, since atom bursts high in the air do add contaminants that possibly affect weather.

Oldtimers accuse the canals in irrigated areas of adding to the humidity and thus to the discomfort. This seems not to be borne out by scientific measurements, but it is undeniably true that cities have changed the weather and even the climate in their vicinity. Perhaps most spectacular of all the artificial changes caused by cities is the smog blanket they spread across skies around the world. Carbon dioxide and water vapor by the thousands of tons are dumped into the air, and both these constituents are known factors in precipitation. Los Angeles smog has teamed with California sunshine to produce great quantities of ozone in the atmosphere, and ozone, too, is a factor in weather.

The idea of weather changing is by no means limited to rainmaking. Russia, not particularly blessed weatherwise over much of its land area, has proposed grandiose schemes for changing the weather in Siberia. All that this would require is the damming of the Bering Strait, and installing giant nuclear-powered pumps to pump warm water so that the coastline would be nicely warmed. Such a scheme sends chills down the spines of

U.S. Department of Commerce

A cloud-seeding airplane operated by the Desert Research Institute. Dry ice is dropped from the open door of the craft to induce precipitation.

Canadians, and even people in the United States wonder what all that melting ice would do to the level of the oceans and to coastal cities.

Over an island in the Mediterranean clouds form downwind because of the heating effect from the land mass. Why not, says the scientist, apply asphalt coatings to large areas of land surface and accomplish the same thing? Or perhaps instead of blacking the land to make it soak up more heat, smooth and brighten it for better reflecting ability. In these ways he proposes to alter the rainfall pattern in the affected areas.

None of these ideas can match in scope those that involve hanging miniature nuclear "suns" in orbit to light up the sky 24 hours a day and to warm cold lands as well. Other proposals include floating miles-long sheets of plastic in the sky for "green-

General Electric

A cloud seeded by Dr. Irving Langmuir near Socorro, New Mexico. Heavy rains fell in the area shortly afterward.

house effect" on the atmosphere, or rigging giant solar reflectors in similar orbits to heat cold spots on the earth below.

Perhaps just such wild ideas prompted the National Science Foundation to release a report early in 1966 labeling environment-tampering as dangerous and on a par with the serious current problems of global war and feeding our expanding population.

In a report issued about the same time, the National Academy of Sciences also pointed out the dangers of inadvertent weather changing, but further stated that weather control is possible. The report suggested more work on weather investigation, and proposed an increase of Federal spending in this direction from the present few million yearly to $50 million a year in the near future.

Forest Service

A ground-based silver-iodide generator for cloud seeding the easy way. This equipment was used by the Forest Service in the Project Skyfire lightning-suppression experiments.

There are various schools of thought on the subject of weather control. We have mentioned von Neumann's view that control might be easier than prediction. Some meteorologists think neither will be possible with real accuracy. These are the men who oppose the deterministic theory that all the factors affecting weather can be analyzed and will then follow through as predicted. Just as the quantum jump cannot be predicted, they say, neither can the weather. It is too complex, too finicky and unstable. On the other hand, some detractors claim just about the opposite: Weather is so stable that puny man even with his nuclear explosives cannot change it significantly.

The weather changers are not at all disheartened by this

This small plane is seeding with dry ice to dispel fog. The service was inaugurated by United Air Lines.

discouragement from their brethren. The fight goes on, and seems to gain strength as it does. Two decades of cloud seeding have not won the war, of course. But with new techniques and equipment, plus better knowledge of what makes weather tick, the weather modifiers will milk rain from reluctant clouds, prevent hail, and maybe even tame tornadoes, hurricanes, and other storms.

"We may achieve climate, but weather is thrust upon us."

—WILLIAM SIDNEY PORTER (O. HENRY)

2

Weather and Climate

ALL of nature reacts to environment. Even nonliving things are susceptible to gravity, the effects of heat and cold, moisture, wind, and the like. Living things are affected in similar manner. Hair stretches when wet, skin turns blue with cold; entire man complains when it is too hot. Doubtless this was one of awakening man's first complaints and it is still Number One on the gripe list. "Everybody talks about the weather," said Charles Dudley Warner (among others), "but nobody does anything about it." The theme of this book belies that defeatist statement, but it has taken thousands of years for humans to move from beings vitally dependent on weather to bold weather makers seeding clouds, chasing fog, and trying to quench the lightning.

Weather and climate were powerful factors in the development of life. Dry-land creatures depended on rainfall, and on temperatures suitable for their metabolism and chemical structure. Gale winds were inimical to feeble life forms. So man flourished in weather that was the best on earth. Yet, perversely, even the best weather constantly thwarts man. Today bad weather spoils things for us; in prehistoric days rain flooded out hunts for food, and refused to fall on new crops. Before we can consider modifying weather for the better, we must know something about it. Fortunately, we know much more than did ancient weather makers.

How Weather Is Made

Life is dependent on the sun for the heat energy to survive; the sun also produces the weather that makes our environment. Ninety-three million miles away, so far that it takes light some eight minutes to reach us, the sun nevertheless is such a tremendous nuclear powerplant that it continually inundates the earth with 250 billion horsepower in the form of heat. Some of this energy bounces off earth's atmosphere, some is reradiated into space by the earth, and some warms man and grows all his food. The remainder provides the motive power for global weather.

Easiest to understand of the sun's contributions to weather is heat. Heat provides the convective force that lifts masses of air vertically. It also provides the energy to evaporate water into vapor that can also be lifted and later released as precipitation. Since three days of solar energy is necessary to produce an inch of rain, it should be obvious that only the tremendous outpouring of heat from the sun could drive the global weather machine.

One problem the first men on the moon will not have is stormy weather. There are no lunar storms because there is no weather at all, as we understand weather, in the airless void surrounding our satellite. Solar heat bakes the moon, and cold space freezes it when night falls, but so far as we know nothing results except on the surface itself. In short, lack of an atmosphere means a lack of weather, no matter how the sun beams down. Earth, however, does have a protective covering of atmosphere tenuously surrounding it, and here is the second needed factor.

There is a third factor, and that is a mixing agent. Were the earth stationary we would have weather, but it would be of a different kind. Half the earth would be frigid with static masses of cold air, and the sunlit half would boil with vertical build-up of cloud which moved horizontally hardly at all. Horizontal winds are necessary to provide global weather patterns, and again the sun comes to the fore. Day and night cause winds primarily by the alternate heating and cooling of land surfaces. The rotation of earth also has something to do with circulation in the great system of trade winds long known and exploited by the sailor. Gravity holds the earth to the sun, and as earth swings in orbit the tilt of its axis produces yet another factor in weather; the increase and decrease in *insolation* that we call summer and winter.

A fourth major factor in weather is water. To be sure, the atmosphere itself constantly contains moisture, in some cases as much as 4 per cent by weight. But there must be a large additional reservoir of water that the atmosphere can draw upon, and into which the rivers can empty, to continue the never-ending hydrologic cycle that is tied tightly with our weather.

We need heat, air, wind, and water for weather. Let us look at the atmosphere in more detail before we put these four elements together and see how the weather factory works.

The Atmosphere

The ancients reckoned four elements: earth, air, fire, water. All of these are important in the weather machine, but the Greeks far underestimated the complexity of air, although the word "atmosphere" does mean "sphere containing vapor." It is common to think of the atmosphere as being a sea of air; that term is used so often we may visualize earth swimming in a huge globe of surrounding atmosphere. Some scientists insist that this is an erroneous concept, and that we should consider the atmosphere more as the peel of an orange or the rind on a melon.

This orange-peel concept takes on validity when we remember that one half of all the molecules in the gaseous atmosphere are below the level of 18,000 feet, or a little more than 3 miles. From here on up the atmosphere thins out gradually so that at an altitude of 55 miles, more than 99 per cent of it is below. For all its seeming lightness, the air that envelops us probably weighs 6 quadrillion tons, with more than a ton pressing down on each square foot at sea level. There are 600 million cubic miles of air, compared to the 250 million cubic miles of water in the seas.

Air, as scientists slowly learned, is not an element itself, but a compound of other elements:

Components of Dry Air

Nitrogen	78.09%
Oxygen	20.95%
Argon	0.93%
Carbon dioxide	0.03%
Neon	trace
Helium	trace
Krypton	trace
Hydrogen	trace
Xenon	trace
Nitrous oxide (laughing gas)	trace
Radon	trace
Methane	trace

There are also two other constituents of the atmosphere most important to weather: dust and water vapor.

Extending about 8 miles from the earth is the region called the *troposphere.* Next is the *stratosphere,* rising to about 30 miles. Then there is the *mesosphere,* which extends to about 55 miles. In a recent new terminology, these three regions are termed the *homosphere,* since the constituents of nitrogen and oxygen remain relatively constant. Above the homosphere is a *heterosphere* of four regions, each characterized by a single element. From 55 miles to 125 miles is a layer of nitrogen. Surrounding the nitrogen layer is a thicker one of oxygen, extending to about 700 miles. Next comes a layer of helium, to 2,200 miles, and finally (it is thought) a layer of hydrogen reaching out to perhaps 22,000 miles.

The atmosphere, then, if we accept the heterosphere as a part of it, really consists of a surrounding sphere of gas some 50,000 miles thick, or almost six times the diameter of the earth it swaddles. Here indeed is a "sea of atmosphere." We shall see later that the interaction of the "solar wind" with the constituents of even the outermost region of this larger atmosphere seems to have an effect on our weather. For now, however, we shall be concerned mostly with the troposphere, the region in which we live and in which most of the meteorological phenomena we call weather take place.

The Circulation of Air Masses

It is easy to create a model of the weather factory; it involves nothing more than a washtub in which water is made to swirl. Basically, it is this simple: The sun shines more directly on the Equator than it does on the poles and thus heats the surface at the Equator more than the poles, as the presence of the icecap indicates. When a land mass—or a water mass, as most of the Equator is—is heated, the air above it is heated too. Heat causes expansion and an increase in the buoyancy of air.

As it rises this heated air moves generally north or south because, in addition to the vertical temperature gradient, there is also a horizontal temperature gradient from the Equator to the poles. The warm air moves poleward and cooler air moves toward the Equator to fill the vacated space. The movement of air is wind, of course, and as cool air moves toward the Equator it acquires a curving direction because of the rotation of the earth. This is the "Coriolis effect," although we are more familiar with the "trade winds" that this effect produces. Such winds blow quite steadily from the northeast in the Northern Hemisphere, and from the southeast south of the Equator.

Earth's rotation also gives rise to other prevailing winds (or lack of winds, as in the doldrums near the Equator). In the temperate zone, where most people in the United States live, we are familiar with prevailing west winds. We fly faster from Los Angeles to New York than in the opposite direction, although time changes may make us think the opposite is true. Farther north are the "polar easterlies" that are not so much a factor in commercial aviation schedules but do figure strongly in the weather picture.

The global wind system, then, sounds quite simple. It is, in theory, and would be in practice also except for the irregularity of land masses, in both a horizontal and a vertical plane. In addition to rotation-induced winds, there are smaller wind systems such as land-sea breezes and mountain-valley winds. The uneven heating of land and water and of different land masses further complicates the mixing pot of weather. Add to this the fact that the atmosphere is alternately heated and cooled from day to night and it is obvious that predicting weather requires more than the simple knowledge that hot air rises, and that winds in the Northern Hemisphere are deflected to the right by the Coriolis effect.

Among regional wind systems are the monsoons of Southeast Asia. Here the wind blows southwest from the sea during the summer and from the northeast in winter. These wind patterns are superimposed upon, or intermingled with, the rotational winds mentioned earlier.

Mountains produce two general kinds of winds: winds that flow upward from the valleys, and katabatic, or downward-flowing, winds. *Foehn,* or *chinook,* winds are literally snow-eaters, and can warm the air temperature as much as 30 degrees in an hour. Los Angeles is familiar with a mountain wind known as the Santa Ana, a hot, dry wind from the east. Opposite of the foehn wind is the *bora,* a cold downward-flowing wind. Boras blow in the mountain country around the Adriatic during winter.

Another wind is a factor in weather, although most of us are unaffected by it directly since it is at such high altitudes. In 1920 U.S. Army Major R. W. Schroder climbed 7 miles high in a plane and was blown far downwind of his takeoff point. Fantastic winds were suspected, and by 1936 a German scientist hypothesized a "jet-stream" wind. However, the jet stream was not verified until World War II, when American bombers raided Japan. Jet streams flow between 25,000 and 40,000 feet, and at speeds higher than 150 miles an hour. Sometimes these snaky ribbons of wind completely circle the earth, but more often are only a few thousand miles long and a few hundred miles wide.

Winds are caused by changes in pressure. Nature seeks equilibrium—although it is sometimes difficult to believe this in the midst of a violent storm—and air moves from a high-pressure area to a low. This is the reason for a variety of winds from the mild sea breeze to the hurricane and tornado. Even unstable air containing little moisture can produce violent winds, as for example the "clear-air turbulence" that sometimes causes "mysterious" airplane crashes. There are also "waves" in the atmosphere, downwind of mountain ranges, that produce turbulence and so-called lenticular, or lens-shaped, clouds.

Three dominant patterns of weather are: planetary waves, which circle the earth at about 20,000 feet; migratory air masses called cyclones (or lows) and anticyclones (or highs); and easterly waves, which cause tropical hurricanes.

The knowledge that air masses and their movements were important in the weather came in the 1920's, through the work of two Norwegian weather scientists, Jakob and Vilhelm Bjerknes. These men suggested that the advance and retreat of masses of air were responsible for the weather over an area. For example, dry, cold air brought clear weather, while moist, warm air was likely to mean clouds and bad weather. Storms occurred where air masses of different composition met, and these meeting lines were called "fronts." Weather systems were found to move about 500 miles a day in summer and 700 miles in winter.

There are four kinds of fronts: cold front, warm front, occluded front, and stationary front. A cold front forms a wedge of air that slides in under warmer air. A warm front rides up over colder air in a kind of inverted wedge. A stationary front is just that, a fixed line between stationary masses of air. When a fast-moving cold front overruns a warm front, the result is a complex frontal structure called an occluded front. Fronts can move as fast as 50 miles an hour.

There are four general air masses in the Northern Hemisphere: continental polar, cold and dry air originating over land; maritime polar, cool and moist air forming over the sea; continental tropical, hot and dry air over land; and maritime tropical, moist and warm air over the sea. Of these four, only continental polar is "stable," or not likely to churn up storms. Jet-stream winds seem to be associated with the movement of the polar front, moving southward when the polar air mass does. Whether this is cause or effect is not yet known, however.

Another approach to weather is that of cyclonic and anticyclonic lows and highs. Winds circling a low-pressure area are termed cyclonic; those about a high are anticyclonic. It seems difficult to tell whether moving air masses cause lows and highs or whether the lows and highs trigger such movement.

Clouds

We noted that the keys to air masses are temperature and humidity. Humidity determines the cloud content of air masses. Three of the air masses are moist, and clouds will form in these three. The word "cloud" is akin to the word "clod" incidentally. Meteorologists have learned over the years that there are many types of clouds, and that their recognition can be an asset in gauging the weather. Frenchman Jean Lamarck and Englishman Luke Howard both suggested systems of classifying clouds at the beginning of the nineteenth century. Howard used the Latin words *cirrus, cumulus,* and *stratus* to begin his cloud glossary, and it received more notice than did Lamarck's, although the latter proposed a similar system.

Cirrus are high, windswept clouds; cumulus the clouds of vertical development; and stratus are horizontal layers, or strata, of clouds. The original three classifications have grown to some thirty-nine divisions, which describe height, shape and structure, and supplementary features of clouds. For instance, *Altocumulus translucidus undulatus* accurately describes a particular cloud type for the meteorologist. Fog is a special designation for cloud in contact with the earth.

As late as the time the first balloon was launched, some people thought clouds were composed of smoke from man-made fires, but meteorologists learned that clouds were drops of water or ice. Most air contains water vapor; if pressure and temperature conditions are right, this vapor is invisible. Warm air can hold more moisture, without being saturated, than cold air. Thus if an air mass is cooled, its water vapor may condense and form water droplets or ice crystals. A cubic yard of heavy cloud contains only $\frac{1}{10}$ ounce of water, but there are so many cubic yards that some 17 trillion tons of water are suspended in the atmosphere! Clouds range in altitude from low-hanging rain clouds to the strange noctilucent clouds observed 50 miles high.

The Structure of Storms

A thunderstorm has its beginnings in a cumulus, the cottony cloud produced by a column or bubble of warmed, rising air. The flat bottom is not produced by the upward pressure of air, as though the cloud were a sort of fleecy balloon, but actually marks the condensation level, the altitude at which air is cooled sufficiently to condense its moisture. Cumulus are generally clouds of good weather, and are welcomed by glider pilots as indicators of lifting currents of air for soaring flight. But if the air is sufficiently unstable and contains enough moisture, ground heating may trigger their growth into the cumulonimbus clouds of thunderstorms.

The formation of water droplets and ice crystals releases heat, and this heat adds to the power of the cloud. More vertical movement then takes place and water droplets grow in size, sometimes freezing into hailstones that are churned up and down inside the thundercloud until they are heavy enough to fall through the powerful updrafts. At maturity the cumulonimbus has rising currents sweeping up around its core and strong downdrafts blowing from its center to the ground where they fan out horizontally in the gusty winds associated with a thunderstorm.

A cumulonimbus can reach up to 60,000 feet, and usually turns into the familiar "anvil-top" of dissipating stratified clouds when the energy of the cloud is used up. The cumulonimbus resembles a nuclear "mushroom" cloud, and the comparison is apt, for the energy expended in a storm can be approximated only by nuclear bombs.

Thunderstorms can be either air-mass storms or frontal storms. We have described the workings of fronts, and how they create storms by mixing different types of air. There are also those that occur within an air mass with no frontal activity involved. These include the simple and generally localized convective thunderstorms, and those caused orographically, by the forcing of moist

balance out the difference. Also, the fair-weather leakage current from earth to atmosphere is observed to be several times as great during auroral activity. The balance of this electrical budget is kept by lightning and other electrical discharge returning what leaks skyward. If the solar wind causes auroral activity and increased electrical leakage to the sky, can reciprocating thunderstorms be far behind?

CLIMATE

Thus far we have talked mostly about weather, and this is understandable since mankind generally discusses weather more than climate. However, we may often mean climate when we complain about rain, heat, or wind. Climate, according to Webster, is "the average course or condition of the weather at a place over a period of years as exhibited by temperature, wind velocity, and precipitation."

It is not weather that makes London cold and foggy, it is climate. It is climate, too, that Robert Frost mentions in a poem describing California, where the environment is such that none ever dies a natural death. "They change their climate, not their disposition, who run beyond the sea," Horace warned two thousand years ago. But disposition seems to hinge to some degree on climate. For further back than Horace, man has sought to change his climate, either by running beyond the sea or changing it locally. Emerson pointed out that coal is a "portable climate" and with furnaces and air-conditioning we have indeed improved our "micro-climates" in homes and buildings.

It has been said in some places notorious for weather, "If you don't like it, wait five minutes." Climate takes longer to change, and it is of greater impact on man, although most of us do not realize this. Climatologist C. E. P. Brooks says:

Practically every action of human life is directly affected by climate. The food we eat, the clothes we wear, the house we dwell in, the work we do, are all dominated by the climate in which we have the good or bad fortune to live.

The city dweller who goes off to work every week-day organizes his life to suit his climate; it is only at week-ends and on holidays that his actions are dominated by the weather (or the weather forecast).

What Makes Climate?

There is a major branch of meteorology called climatology, which is concerned with the physical state of the atmosphere during specified periods of time and within specified geographic areas. In its broadest aspect climate may be considered on a global scale, and actually this is the simplest way to consider it. The heat intake and heat loss of the earth, as well as the total amount of moisture in circulation, is known. For a smaller portion of the globe, however, these factors are not constant but change greatly from time to time.

As with weather, two basic factors make climate. These are the heat, or insolation, received from the sun, and the earth itself with its surrounding atmosphere and various terrestrial features including seas, plains, mountains, deserts, and so on.

The output of heat from the sun has been determined to be fairly constant. In fact, that term is applied to its radiation as received on earth. "The solar constant," defined as the radiation reaching earth (outside its atmosphere) when earth is at the mean distance from the sun, is 1.94 gram-calories per square centimeter per minute. To convert this into a more meaningful figure, about 1,000 watts of solar power strike a square yard of surface placed at right angles to the sun's rays; this is equivalent to about $1\frac{1}{3}$ horsepower!

Since earth swings about the sun in an elliptical orbit that is not a perfect circle, it is at times farther away from the sun. At aphelion, or the closest point to the sun, earth has a radiation intake of 2.01 gram calories per square centimeter per minute. Aphelion, incidentally, takes place early in January, when we experience our cold weather. At perihelion, when the sun is farthest away, the radiation received falls to 1.86. This is early in July. Annual variations are less than 1 per cent, so the sun shines steadily.

The reason winters are colder despite more heat received is the
23½-degree tilt of the earth's axis of rotation. This results in the
rays of the sun striking us at more of a slant in winter than in
summer. The tilt of the earth is actually a compensating factor
for its elliptical orbit. Without both we would have greater
extremes in weather.

Thus far we have considered the earth as a sphere receiving all
the energy it intercepts. This is not the case, because of various
reasons. The earth, fortunately for us, has an atmosphere, which
screens out much harmful radiation. It also reflects or absorbs
about 57 per cent of the radiation from the sun. This is an
average figure, and on clear days 80 per cent of the radiation may
reach the earth, while on very cloudy days only 30 per cent gets
through the atmosphere.

Of the average 43 per cent of the radiation which does reach
earth, not all is absorbed as heat. The reflection coefficient, which
scientists call the *albedo,* of earth varies from 5 per cent to 20 per
cent, depending on whether it is icecap or dark, rough earth.
Average albedo is about 12 per cent, so only 88 per cent of
received heat is absorbed. Thus only a little more than one-third
(or 43 per cent less 12 per cent) of the sun's heat is absorbed by
earth.

Earth itself radiates heat too. Part of this is reradiated solar
heat, and part is radioactive heat from earth's crust. Some of this
heat is trapped in the atmosphere, mainly by particles of carbon
dioxide and dust, but some escapes to outer space. In spite of
these complexities, climatologists are able to plot the net radiation for earth.

Rotation of the earth is constant, and the moisture in the air
and the circulation of wind generally adhere to patterns that can
be relied upon. These factors give climate to areas of the globe.
In the tropics it is hot, at the polar caps it is cold. Over the
oceans and coastal areas of continents, the air contains more
moisture than it does over inland regions. A plain downwind of a
range of mountains receives less rain than the mountain. The
following are the various kinds of climates: hot monsoon, Mediterranean, desert, temperate, and cold.

The effect of climate on life is obvious, and among the formal "rules" of climate are: *Allen's Rule:* Protruding body parts are relatively shorter in cooler climates; *Bergmann's Rule:* The size of mammals increases toward the poles; and *Gloger's Rule:* Climate affects the color of mammals and birds.

As early as 1686 Robert Hooke theorized that climate had once been much warmer. By 1778 Buffon suggested a cooling earth in which life-forms gradually retreated from the poles. German botanist K. F. Schimper in 1829 introduced the term "ice age," and a decade later Poisson talked of earth having moved through "cold regions" in space to produce the chilling of the ice age.

In earth's long history there have been drastic climatic changes. Its change from a fiery ball of gas to the present rather tepid state of affairs must have been marked by stormy ups and downs that featured great ice ages that came and passed. The last of these strange freezes, during which glaciers advanced from the north, waned sometime before the sixth millennium B.C. Scientists know this because about 6000 B.C. the continental climate of Europe—hot summers and cold winters—began to change to a warm humid climate. Rainfall was much heavier than at present, and temperature was probably 5 degrees Fahrenheit warmer, since there was a considerable growth of peat in the area. This period is known as the Climatic Optimum. In Scandinavia the land masses subsided and water from the warm Atlantic enlarged the Baltic Sea. Studies of the flora of Spitsbergen from this early period suggest that the Arctic Ocean was then free of ice.

Following the Climatic Optimum, Europe underwent a gradual decrease of rainfall and a drop in temperature, with occasional long droughts followed by relatively brief increases in precipitation. There were dry periods from 2200 to 1900 B.C., 1200 to 1000 B.C. and 700 to 500 B.C. The last 200-year drought is thought to have been a dry heat wave, and led to migrations of people to wetter regions.

After 500 B.C. there was a change in a relatively short time to a wetter and colder climate, perhaps the change referred to in literature as the "twilight of the gods." Peat grew rapidly enough to kill off the forests in large areas. Lakes in the Alpine regions

rose and wiped out many settlements. Within 500 years, however, the rain again decreased and temperature rose to about
what is being experienced now in Europe.

Again in the seventeenth century Europe experienced a climatic change in the "Little Ice Age." Since it is doubtful that
man was at that time tampering with the climate on a broad
scale, scientists assume that this sudden dropping of temperatures
was caused naturally. They are unable to determine these causes,
however. Because of this inability, despite the recentness of the
event and the availability of data, it is assumed that very subtle
changes in temperature, moisture, or other factors were to blame.

A much more recent climatological change is the apparent
worldwide warming that has occurred during the last 50 to 65
years, a warming that has increased Arctic winter temperatures as
much as 3 degrees Centigrade. There is an even longer observed
trend toward decreasing precipitation in the United States, the
northern part of South America, Africa, Malaysia, and Australia,
and an increase in precipitation in the Arctic, the North Temperate Zone, Mexico, La Plata, southern India, and Southeast
Asia. These changes have been detected by checking records back
to 1885.

Sunspots are often blamed for changes in climate. Astrophysi-
cist C. G. Abbot, among those who have advanced such theories,
found an eleven-year cycle in climate, corresponding to the
sunspot cycles. Climatologist H. Wexler also believes there is a
correlation between sunspot activity and climate change. He says
that an increase in the content of carbon dioxide in the atmosphere, and a reduction of the amount of volcanic ash also may
have an effect. The increased carbon dioxide is largely due to
man's industries; the second to the lessening volcanic activity in
the last 50 years.

Studies of the reduction of solar radiation caused by the
eruption of Alaska's Katmai volcano in 1912 showed that 20 per
cent less solar energy reached earth for a brief period thereafter.
A cold winter followed the eruption of Katmai, and it has been
pointed out that similar cold waves followed the eruption of
Asama in Japan in 1783, Tamboro in the East Indies in 1815,

and Krakatoa in Indonesia in 1883. Even further back, an Icelandic saga of the thirteenth century refers to eruptions and cold weather. However, the volcano Conseguina in Nicaragua produced no noticeable effect on the weather.

It seems obvious that if the heat intake of an area is changed the climate will be changed too. Likewise, if the natural course of winds is altered, climate will be different. And massive as the task might seem, it is easier in principle to change climate than weather.

To review, weather is caused by the sun, by the land and water surfaces the sun shines upon, by the rotation of earth and its revolution about the sun, and by moisture in the air. Weather includes temperature, precipitation, wind, and lightning.

Climate is weather on a long-range basis. There is evidence on much of the earth of climate change, with some areas hotter and drier than formerly. Man himself may have made more changes in climate than he has been able to effect on weather, by burning off and otherwise using timber, by loading the air with smog, and by altering temperature and wind with his cities.

"Probable nor'east to sou'-west winds, varying to the southard and westard and eastard and points between; high and low barometer, sweeping round from place to place; probable areas of rain, snow, hail, and drought, succeeded or preceded by earthquakes with thunder and lightning."

—MARK TWAIN

3

Predicting the Weather

IN a magazine article in 1954, Captain Howard T. Orville, USN (Retired), wrote:

I think it entirely probable that, in 10 years, your daily weather forecast will read something like this:

"Freezing rain, starting at 10:46 A.M., ending at 2:32 P.M." or, "Heavy snowfall, seven inches, starting at 1:43 A.M., continuing throughout day until 7:37."

And the weather will adhere to that time schedule. Jokes about the weatherman's predictions will be obsolete, because his forecasts, based on an elaborate electronic system of reporting and analyzing data, will admit of no error.

Weatherman jokes are still with us, of course, and 1964 came and passed with no such accurate forecasts as those expected by Captain Orville, who was, at the time he made the prediction, chairman of the Advisory Committee on Weather Control. Yet weather prediction has made great advances in the years since 1954. In fact, British authorities have complained of late that not nearly enough use is being made by industry and agriculture of accurate and useful prediction of coming weather. If such use were made, they argue, savings amounting to millions of dollars could be made.

Such an admission should be encouraging to those who would change the weather, since accurate prediction has been called a prerequisite for useful control of weather. Let us see, then, the present state of the gentle art of foretelling the weather.

THE NEED FOR WEATHER PREDICTION

Since most of us are going to grumble about the weather no matter how it turns out, it might seem a waste of time and money trying to guess in advance what is coming. Why know that a heat wave is going to make life miserable? There are a hundred and more reasons, of course, why we want to know what the weatherman has in store.

While it has not been proved that wars cause weather, it is obvious from history that weather has won and lost wars. Napoleon lost in Russia and elsewhere when the weather was against him. Later, Napoleon Bonaparte would ask Urbain Leverrier, the astronomer who discovered Neptune, to investigate a storm that had wrecked a French fleet. Leverrier announced that it might have been possible to foretell this storm by means of weather reports along its path. By World War II the accurate prediction of weather was a conclusive factor in victory, as proved when the Allies invaded Normandy on the strength of good forecasting. The Germans were caught with their predictions down, thinking that the weather would be too bad for such a move.

Aviation generally, and the airlines in particular, must know what is ahead weatherwise, as indeed must other forms of transport, including ships. Contractors affected by the weather work closely with the weatherman, as do movie producers and all photographers. Power companies, farmers, and city managers all want to know the weather ahead so that they may plan accordingly.

Sporting events held outside are dependent on the weather.

Businesses selling fur coats and air-conditioning plants are too. Less obviously dependent on the weather are industries like canning-jar manufacturing, but these businesses need to know where and when crops will be ripening and canned by professionals and home canners.

The business of weather forecasting, then, is one of great importance. America's first official forecaster was Increase Lapham, and his first predictions in 1870 warned of strong winds on the Great Lakes, one of the main reasons for establishing a weather service having been to alert shippers.

There is another important reason for learning to predict the weather accurately. Man switched from trying to change the weather to predicting it only because he could not do the former. It is good to be able to predict the coming hurricane or freeze, but how much better it would be to ward it off, to change it to weather more kindly to man and animals. Certainly weather prediction is of an importance far greater than just foretelling weather conditions—it is the scientific base for intelligent modification of weather and climate on a large scale.

EARLY WEATHERMEN

Man boldly began his bout with weather by attempting to change it with magic. With the wisdom of experience he finally began to wonder if maybe just knowing what was ahead might be a worthy compromise. So one of the earliest of the seers, the weather prognosticator, developed. Earlier than 1000 B.C. there were seers in Babylon, and also priests smart enough to denounce as frauds those who predicted the weather a year in advance. Cuneiform writings show that as early as 700 B.C. public weather predictors were on the Assyrian payroll.

Some of the pioneers in weather prediction used methods that seem to have no connection at all with the actual factors controlling weather. For instance augurs sacrificed chickens and other animals and poked in the entrails to find signs indicating rain or drought.

Perhaps somewhat more scientific were predictions based on vegetation:

> Onion's skin very thin:
> Mild winter coming in.
> Onion's skin thick and tough:
> Coming winter cold and rough.

Insects and animals too were—and are—favorite clues or cues for the coming weather:

> When eager bites the thirsty flea,
> Clouds and rain you sure shall see.
>
> When the glowworm lights his lamp,
> Then the air is always damp.
>
> Before the storm, the crab his briny home
> Sidelong forsakes and strives on land to roam.
>
> If spiders their cobwebs forsake
> The weather will for certain break.

Snails were omens of bad weather too, as were leeches and frogs. When frogs remained in their pools, for example, the weather would be fine. If they came up on the rocks rain and cold would follow. One last poem concerning animal weather signs, which may or may not have been intended seriously:

> Hark, I hear the asses bray;
> Methinks we'll have some rain today!

The lesser creatures may instinctively know more of weather than does man, but some men were learning to bypass the animal intermediaries and read signs directly. In the Bible Elihu tells Job, "Out of the south cometh the whirlwind and cold out of the north." And in Aristophanes' play *The Clouds* a character makes a pointed remark concerning weather: "That's not Zeus up there, but a vortex of air."

Aristotle wrote the first book on weather—it included astronomy too—and entitled it *Meteorologica,* meaning "the study of things above." Aristotle believed that when hot dry air was heated by the sun it rose and ignited the fiery component of the atmosphere, producing wind, thunder, and lightning. He also believed that comets, meteors, and auroras were caused by this heating, an erroneous assumption, of course. He also said that rising moist air entering the airy component of space caused clouds and precipitation, a quite sound judgment. His theory of the hydrologic cycle, the evaporation of water from the ocean, and its precipitation and eventual return to the sea, was also accurate and is accepted by modern hydrologists.

Unfortunately, but understandably, Aristotle's book was not completely reliable. For example, he stated that the east winds were warmer because the sun shown in the east longer. Even in the time of Pliny the Elder, the Roman writer who died in 79 A.D., it was still believed that the winds originated in caves of the earth.

With all the errors and fallacies, however, there were some shrewd observations of weather based on animals and other things. Predictions based on the roosting habits of birds, which are affected by slight physical changes in the atmosphere, or on the colors of the sunset or the ring around the moon, for example, have some validity. There were more ambitious looks at the sky, and weather was ascribed not only to the sun but to other stars and the planets as well.

Aristotle believed that weather could be predicted by simply looking at the sky overhead. To some extent this is true, but it is also like trying to prevent accidents by looking up at the truck that runs over you. Advance warning would be a welcome thing, and only when it was realized that weather is a global matter, and what happens in distant lands affects weather at home, was progress made in accurate weather prediction.

After Aristotle there was a long lull in weather prediction of an intelligent nature. Other Greeks generally turned to their gods for guidance, and elsewhere weather prediction leaned on such things as astrology.

Astrology and god-lore finally gave way to earthier bases for weather forecasting. The first of the almanacs was *Prognostica,* appearing in Europe about the beginning of the sixteenth century. Here was weather predicted a year ahead on the basis of shrewd guesswork or perhaps even the toss of a coin. But ignorant and gullible people bought the almanacs by the thousands. American colonists brought them over and by 1792 the most famous of all, the old *Farmer's Almanac,* was in print. It is still being published today and is a tribute to the tongue-in-cheek acceptance of its subscribers, and the good-humored "science" of the men who prepare it.

SCIENTIFIC PREDICTION

Studying the bark on trees and the stripes on a caterpillar might be more scientific than eyeing the liver of a sacrificial lamb, but this was still not true meteorology. The real science had to wait for accurate methods of measuring the factors involved in the making of weather. First came Leonardo da Vinci's wind vane, more accurate than the early Greek parapegmata, or wind indicator. The next such piece of equipment was the thermometer, invented by Galileo about 1593. His later invention, the telescope, would one day also figure in the study of weather, but the thermometer, which measured temperature of air and liquids, first helped the fledgling science of weather.

In 1643 Galileo's student Torricelli invented the barometer, an instrument for measuring the pressure of air. Less than twenty years later an Irishman named Robert Boyle propounded his law concerning the relationship between the volume of a gas and the pressure applied to it, a basic law in the dynamics of the atmosphere. In 1667 the Englishman Robert Hooke invented the anemometer for measuring the speed of the wind.

Later a clever weather-forecasting machine was built using nothing but a barometer. Air pressure caused a needle to move to fair weather, falling pressure moved it to stormy weather. This fascinating robot was actually fairly accurate, and is still in use. One version has wooden figures which come forth from a tiny cottage in response to changing weather conditions.

Looking far ahead of his time was Ferdinand II, Grand Duke of Tuscany. This ruler established several meteorological stations in various places in Italy in 1653. Not only did he promote such a "national" system, but even advocated an international organization of weather stations. It was not until 1780, however, that the Meteorological Society of the Palatinate began to operate, with standard rain gauges used by German, Swiss, Austrian, and American meteorologists. The observation and recording of American weather data was begun in Charleston, South Carolina, by a physician in 1670.

The seventeenth century continued to be a big one for the infant science of weather. The English mathematician Edmund Halley in 1686 published the first accounts of the trade winds and monsoons, based on his two years at sea, and a decade later adventurer William Dampier published his book on ocean winds that was useful to sea captains for a hundred years.

Thus far the weatherman had been tied to the ground in making his measurements. Even those readings of temperature and pressure and humidity taken by mountaineers were not true for free air at that altitude because the mountain itself altered the physiology of the atmosphere. What was needed was a means of taking the pulse of weather high in the air where it actually developed, and in 1749 two curious Scotsmen tied a thermometer to the tail of a kite and sent it aloft for the first true readings of temperature at altitude. Another and more famous kite experiment came just three years later when Benjamin Franklin put one up into a storm and tapped electricity from a lightning bolt.

A kite was fine, but there was a limit to the amount of string one could use and to the horizontal distance covered as well. In 1783, the Montgolfier brothers in France produced the first man-carrying balloon, and this gas bag was soon lifting men and instruments high into the sky and all over the countryside. More or less accurate plots of air pressure, temperature, and winds aloft began to emerge as these daredevils clung to swaying gondolas and occasionally lost their lives. In 1809 an Englishman named Thomas Forster launched the first small, unmanned weather balloons. By watching their course from the ground, he was able to plot information on upper wind currents.

What did the scientist have now, as far as meteorological know-how was concerned? He could measure the pertinent factors of temperature, pressure, humidity, and wind speed. He could guess how these factors worked together to produce clouds or clear weather or precipitation, but he was still hamstrung as far as really predicting the weather. He could make his readings and then say it is raining, or the sun is shining. But so could someone standing ankle deep in that rain, or baking in the sunshine. Accurate scientific prediction was not yet possible. It was not enough to know weather conditions right overhead; knowledge was needed of the factors over a wide area.

When Halley published his weather maps, from which the meteorologist could see relationships between global conditions and weather, all this was after the fact, and of only academic interest. Even when Benjamin Franklin followed up his kite experiment with the discovery that weather moved generally from southwest to northeast this important news was of no practical value. Weather moved faster than man could travel, and so there was no way of getting the word ahead. The weatherman was like a prisoner aboard a steamroller moving to flatten his home—he couldn't leap off and get the word there in time because the steamroller traveled faster than he did. Not until the middle of the nineteenth century would this handicap be overcome.

George Hadley advanced a basic theory for the trade winds, stating that they were the result of earth's rotation as well as the heating of tropical air and resultant upward movement. Here was a step forward, but the beginnings of real weather fore- casting came about 1820 when the German meteorologist Hein- rich Wilhelm Brandes produced the synoptic chart. "Synoptic" derives from Greek words meaning "a seeing together." In other words, synoptic weather charts are based on an examination of weather at a number of locations simultaneously, with the reali- zation that weather is not a local occurrence but part of the whole global system. Englishman Francis Galton, who pioneered a number of fields including eugenics, fingerprinting, and ultra- sonics, also did work in the simultaneous charting of weather.

There was one serious flaw in the early synoptic chart: it could not be converted into a weather forecast soon enough to be of use.

Early weather forecasters spun their wheels as far as any immediate good was apparent. It took a long time to collect the weather observations from a number of points, making it hopeless to use this data in forecasting weather. Of course, the forecaster could go ahead and make an after-the-fact forecast and then check it against what had really come from the heavens. Here at least was a test of the validity of the idea that weather was forecastable. Adding the time necessary for collecting data to time required for analyzing resulted in a long delay and a forecast of only scientific interest. Yet only on such patient and selfless work of early weathermen could real forecasting be based.

The pattern of weather was beginning to be seen. By 1841 the American meteorologist James Pollard Epsy showed that local air temperatures were closely related to the general conditions of the atmosphere. In 1849 he made a report for the United States Navy which traced the movement of "cyclonic" wind systems across America. His maps also depicted what we now know as weather fronts. And by 1856 William Ferrell gave meteorology the theory of the general circulation of the atmosphere. Chiefly needed now was a communication system fast enough to exploit man's knowledge of weather conditions at various stations. And fortunately that system was already at hand.

Just as the invention of the kite and then the balloon had aided earlier, another invention in the middle of the nineteenth century boomed the weather-prediction business. Samuel Morse tapped the message "What hath God wrought?" from Washington to Baltimore in 1844. This message, which could as well have read "It is raining here," covered the distance faster than any horse and rider ever could; faster than any storm. Electricity like that of the storm's lightning flashed through wires almost instantaneously. Now the weatherman had his long-needed communications link.

By 1850 there were 150 telegraph stations sending weather data to the Smithsonian Institution in Washington, a kind of central clearinghouse for weather information. These reports actually took precedence over death notices. Soon almost-current weather maps were being published both in the United States and in Europe. This was a far cry from the pioneer efforts of Halley, who had produced a map that was two years out-of-date when he was finally able to set down all the information gathered on his long and tedious globe-girdling ocean trip. By 1860 there were 500 stations reporting in the United States, Canada, and Paraguay.

Unfortunately, immediate success did not reward the weathermen. In London the chief of the weather office furnished weather predictions to the newspapers, to the embarrassment of the Royal Society. When the chief died in 1865 the Society quickly canceled the predictions, or "anticipations" as they had been called, and they were not reinstated for about fifteen years.

In America, President Abraham Lincoln was unimpressed by the prognostications of weathermen, and declined their suggestions for a national weather service. Not until 1870 was such a service created, and then it was merely an adjunct of the Army's Signal Service, a branch that would later have the additional honor of nurturing the first air force for the country.

Understandably, early weather predictions were not 100 per cent accurate. As late as 1900 the *Denver Republican* was publishing a weekly weather forecast made by Oliver Wiggins, a former frontier scout who depended on an old battle wound for his predictions! Embarrassingly, Wiggins often correctly foretold the weather when the official forecast did not, and weathermen pleaded with the paper to move Wiggins' unofficial forecast to another page.

This ability to forecast weather through physical discomfort was celebrated in numerous poems like this one:

> A coming storm your shooting corns presage,
> And aches will throb, your hollow tooth will rage.

In 1891 the weather stations were transferred from the Signal Service to the Department of Agriculture, itself a new organization. In 1940, the National Weather Service moved again and changed its name. Its new home was the Department of Commerce and it was called the United States Weather Bureau. In 1965, the Department of Commerce created a new agency called

Environmental Science Services Administration (ESSA), composed of the Weather Bureau and other Government weather services.

As we have seen, the coming of the telegraph in the mid-1800's solved part of the problem of speedy and practical synoptic forecasting. But there was still the almost insurmountable prob-

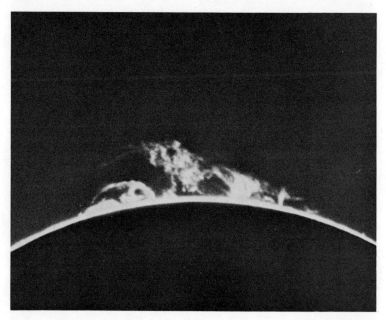

W. Orr Roberts

The sun—author of our weather.

lem of doing the necessary mathematics to reduce thousands of observations of temperature, pressure, humidity, wind speed, and direction.

World War I proved a blessing in disguise to meteorology. Norway, which was neutral in that conflict, was cut off from weather reports of other nations. To fill the gap, she instituted a network of stations, closely spaced and reporting regularly.

Vilhelm and Jakob Bjerknes coupled such data with a new theory of weather to produce the first accurate and practical forecasting system. After the war the Norwegian system was adopted around the world and was a tremendous stride toward fast and accurate forecasting.

Radio helped the fledgling weather stations, and so did the follow-on to the balloon: the airplane. The airplane was one of those vital developments that both created new prediction techniques and demanded them as well: weather was of prime importance to the flier. As scheduled flights began to be made, pilots were still relying on scanty weather forecasts, some of them based on kite-borne measuring equipment. Charles Lindbergh was among the pilots who refused to rely on weather forecasts from the Bureau but judged the weather en route. Some pilots made it a habit to land and phone ahead to ask farmers how the weather was in the next county.

Part of the new era in weather forecasting for aircraft was use of the aircraft itself as a weather-data collector. In 1931 the Weather Bureau was hiring pilots to fly daily from Chicago, Cleveland, Omaha, and Dallas, logging the weather. High altitude was the aim of these flights, and pay did not start until 13,500 feet was reached. For each additional 1,000 feet, $25 was paid.

Now the weatherman had the benefit of accurate measurements at altitudes of interest to the pilot, plus the bonus of better forecasts for groundbound humans too. The base altitude for weather flights was raised eventually to 16,500 feet with better aircraft, and ten cities were included in the network. In the late 1930's, however, weathermen began using balloons equipped with radio and measuring gear. This was the radiosonde, and it put most high-flying weather pilots out of business.

For soundings higher than a plane or a balloon could reach, the rocket was put to use and eventually placed satellites in orbit where constant surveillance of the weather was possible. Edmund Halley cruised for years gathering data for a weather map; now weather satellites provide instantaneous coverage of the weather picture around the world. Where once the weatherman had to put together his maps by laboriously combining bits of data from reporting stations all over the world, now he can see the weather as it really is from his satellite vantage point hundreds of miles above earth's surface.

Tiros and other weather satellites aid greatly in getting information to the weatherman, with television pictures of the cloud coverage of the earth available almost immediately. ESSA 2, a weather satellite of the Environmental Science Services Administration, sends back pictures from 800 miles, permitting a view of the entire cloud coverage of half the world at a glance.

Another powerful tool available to the weatherman today is the computer, which can perform in just a single minute the work of 1,000 meteorologists working with desk calculators for 24 hours.

There are 25,000 weathermen in the United States; globally there are an estimated 5 million full and part-time weathermen. There are 600 upper-air observation stations in existence, of which 200 are in America. Robot weather stations are located in various places, some of them anchored at sea and automatically observing and reporting the conditions in the area. A suggestion has been made to create a fleet of thousands of radio-instrumented constant-level balloons floating at different altitudes in the sky and to be interrogated regularly by orbiting satellites.

The complete answer to weather forecasting is full coverage of global weather by weather stations, and as yet we are far short of such coverage. However, international cooperation is doing much to remedy this defect in the weather-forecasting network.

How Forecasts Are Made

Weather prediction is for the wise, the brave, or the foolish. We have always had a number in each category willing to stick their meteorological necks out, and methods of prediction are as varied as the successes achieved. During the 1850's, with a beginning of scientific prediction in synoptic charts and telegraphic communication, there was still the "Sage of Brooklyn Heights" who boldly issued his amateur long-range weather forecasts, going far beyond the time span attempted by the official weatherman. Mr. Dooley, of literary fame, relied on Clancy's ailing leg as his forecast guide. And often these unscientific weathermen seemed more accurate than Uncle Sam's specialists.

In 1909, for example, Weather Bureau chief Willis L. Moore issued a forecast of "clear and colder" for the inauguration of President William Howard Taft. When it snowed instead, enemies of Moore used his inaccuracy as the basis for an attack on his position. Circulars were distributed in 1919 in Grand Rapids, Michigan, attacking the entire Weather Bureau:

The Weather Bureau is a humbug and grafting outfit. To hell with it. If you are honest and work for a living, you don't want to pay for what man don't have anything to do with. The weather is God's business only.

Not only the unlettered, but the lawmakers as well, derided the Weather Bureau. Congressman William S. Howard of Georgia wanted the Bureau abolished, and preferred an acquaintance of his who used a sourwood stick instead of synoptic charts to make his predictions!

The advance of scientific weather prediction continued, however, and was even foretold in poetic folklore. Such jingles as

> Red sky at morning, sailors take warning,
> Red sky at night, sailors delight,

and

> Mackerel skies and mares' tails
> Make lofty ships carry low sails,

took into account the fact that weather moved from east to west, and that clouds were trusty indicators of weather. There are many other commonsense statements of this nature:

> The weather is like news:
> It travels on the wind.

> It rains for as long
> As it takes to come.

Rain before seven,
Clear before eleven.

Weather poets seem always pessimistic; for example, these
rhymes:

The farther the sight
The nearer the rain.

A good hearing day
Is a sign of wet.

If the moon rises hallowed 'round,
Soon you'll tread on deluged ground.

But then it is mostly bad weather that concerns us; in fact, to
the meteorologist weather is generally something else than a
beautifully clear day.

Two differing philosophical views on weather are expressed in
the following quotations:

Rain, rain, go away
Come again some other day.

If God wills, rain comes with any wind.

It happens that there are also two opposing views concerning
weather forecasting, or prediction; the "statistical" approach,
and "numerical weather prediction."

Statistical Weather Forecasting

Just as many sciences are based on statistical behavior—such as
the elections that are part of political science—some weathermen
insist that only the statistical approach can yield accurate predictions of local weather. This is the dynamic, or analog, method
in which the meteorologist compares present weather conditions
with those that have prevailed in the past, and bases his prediction on what such conditions led to. For example, moisture and
winds often lead to rainy weather. So does a drop in pressure, as
we know from home barometers that are marked fair or stormy.
Thus a statistical prediction is based on what will probably

happen, and generally is expressed in percentages. There is a 50-50 chance for showers—or for clear weather.

The word "probable" is increasingly associated with weather forecasts. "A 20 per cent probability for light showers in the evening hours." "A 30 per cent probability that the temperature will dip below freezing in the early morning." Weather forecasts should be interpreted in this light, then. Although short-range weather forecasts are today about 75 per cent to 85 per cent accurate, there is the 15 per cent to 25 per cent of misses that must be allowed for. This statistical prediction is the natural outcome of a method based on statistical probabilities rather than determinism.

Statistical weather forecasting has been defined as the prediction of weather by rules based upon the statistics of weather behavior. Such forecasting considers the present state of the weather and expected changes in physical conditions in the future. As an aid, the meteorologist usually refers to records on the behavior of the atmosphere previously under similar conditions.

Modern meteorologists base their predictions on observations of physical conditions of the atmosphere and a more or less learned extrapolation of those conditions some hours into the future. Some observations of conditions require no instruments but only the good eye of the weatherman. Visibility, for instance, and the amount and type of cloud cover. Present weather, plus a memory of that in the recent past, is pertinent to prediction.

Instrumented observations include barometric pressure of the air, and the tendency of that pressure, whether rising, falling, or prevailing. Temperature, humidity, cloud height, wind speed, and direction—all these can be measured by instruments available to the weatherman.

Now for the projection into the future of the observed condition of atmospheric factors that make weather. Over the years weathermen have learned a number of empirical rules of prediction. One of these is the "continuity" of weather, the fact that weather should continue much as it is for 12 to 24 hours unless a low or a front passes or approaches. Furthermore, any lows or fronts approaching should move at the same speed for the next 12- to 24-hour period as they did in the past period of that length.

Ordinarily, the larger a storm area, the more slowly it moves. Season affects this speed, however, as does local terrain. For example, in summer and at sea, lows move at an average speed of 30 to 35 miles an hour. Highs move some 10 miles an hour slower. Irregular terrain may lop 20 miles from these speeds. Winter adds 5 to 10 miles an hour to average speeds of moving pressure areas.

Low-pressure areas move toward dropping pressures, away from rising pressures. Lows also move in the direction of upper air flow, and this flow is in the same direction as surface flow but faster. Also, the higher into the atmosphere a low reaches, the slower it moves.

According to one writer on weather, "Old weather never dies, it just changes form." The statistical forecaster is a master at knowing the present form of weather and scientifically "guesstimating" the speed and magnitude of changes that will occur. For weather further ahead than 48 hours, such subjective forecasts remain more accurate. But a more modern weather-prognostication technique is doing battle with the long-established empirical method of statistical forecasting.

Numerical Weather Prediction

Until the 1920's the forecasting of weather was done on an empirical basis. Weathermen knew that certain conditions generally led to weather of one kind. For example, low pressure and moisture are indicators of rain. This "qualitative" forecasting dominated when meteorologist Lewis R. Richardson suggested a more exact method in 1922.

Richardson's idea stemmed from his belief that given certain meteorological conditions, he could mathematically derive the resulting weather. Here was "quantitative" analysis; *how much* rain for *how long,* rather than the mere forecast of rain sometime in the future. The tools for such numerical analysis of the

weather were available in the partial differential equations de-
rived by the Swiss mathematician Leonhard Euler. These so-
called "primitive equations" involved wind velocity, density,
pressure, temperature, and other factors.

Richardson's plan was to predict the weather for much of

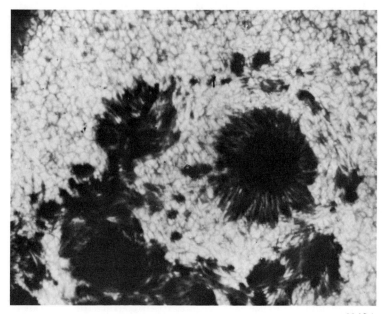

NASA

Sunspots, the strange outbreaks on the solar surface that affect earth's
weather 93 million miles distant.

England 24 hours ahead by analyzing reports from many stations.
He actually did so, and fairly accurately. But the old fly was still
in the meteorological ointment: Richardson had to work for
three months to produce his forecast and it was ancient history
by the time he had it completed.

It was estimated that 1,000 meteorologists, each with a desk
calculator, would require 24 hours to produce a forecast one hour

in advance. Richardson himself decided that if he could have the services of 60,000 mathematicians he might make his scheme work, but such an operation would be so costly that England still had to do without knowing the weather accurately a day in advance.

Indirectly, another war aided weather prediction. In 1945 the first electronic computer was produced to aid the United States war effort. By 1950 a more advanced computer was cranking out just the kind of information that Richardson had dreamed of three decades before. Substituting a simpler "Rossby equation," named for Professor C. G. Rossby with only four terms that combined the more complex Euler equations, computermen John von Neumann and Julian Bigelow fed in reports from 768 weather stations. In 48 minutes the computer performed 30 million operations and produced a 24-hour forecast.

Fed into the computer were the atmospheric pressure level readings for a grid of stations covering the United States and Canada. At first the readings for one pressure level, or altitude, were used, but this was doubled later, and led to a noticeable improvement in accuracy. The stations reporting were about 300 kilometers (about 180 miles) apart. Jule Charney, working with von Neumann, increased the computer input to six levels of readings, the "intellectual capacity" of the numerical system at that time.

Let us look now at the mechanics of such a task and how the team of meteorologist and computer can convert the millions of bits of weather data into an automatically printed weather report for 24 hours from now.

There are four things necessary for successful numerical weather prediction: sufficient data for all parts of the world's weather; a knowledge of how physical conditions of the weather change into other conditions; a means of putting this information into the proper form; and rapid processing to get the needed results. As yet, all four conditions are not ideally met, but there is progress. New observational methods including radar techniques, rocket soundings, and weather satellites have yielded more information and a better understanding of how weather is made. Improved mathematical techniques and the advent of the electronic computer have done much to fulfill the last two requirements.

Although the mathematics of differential equations, even in the simpler Rossby form, are beyond the scope of this book, the basic method of approach can be discussed. The air is treated as a frictionless fluid moving over a rotating plane, and enough data is fed into the computer about its velocity, pressure, and so on. This yields information on the motions of waves in the atmos-

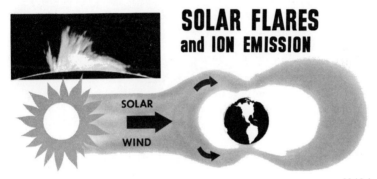

NASA

The solar wind that causes changes in the earth's weather.

phere. At present this information is of a rather general nature and applies to very large areas of air mass, and for periods of from one to three days.

Similar equations can be run through the computer to find what will happen in the future with respect to clouds and precipitation. Here the pertinent factors are humidity and temperature.

The U.S. Navy first made numerical weather prediction a reality in NANWEP (NAvy Numerical WEather Prediction). Today information from 3,000 stations is given to the computer and it prints out a 24-hour forecast in 40 minutes.

Obviously the work required for longer forecast periods is much greater. For example, a 24-day forecast by numerical analysis requires 10 billion operations of the computer; a 100-day forecast more than a trillion! This is still a dream; today 3-day forecasts are made by computer.

It is thought that the numerical prediction method will prove of value in predicting climate before it is practical for predicting short-range weather fluctuations for extended periods. Computers with from 100 to 1,000 times the capacity of present models may be needed for really accurate long-range predictions of local weather.

The determinists are every bit as confident of their methods as are the statistical-approach meteorologists. They recognize the need for more accurate indicators to supplement strictly theoretical calculations, and suggest that the jet stream may be just such an indicator. And to track the jet stream there are certain cloud formations present most of the time the jet stream is active. The jet stream seems to indicate the movement of planetary waves important in global weather.

In 1953, Dr. Rossby suggested a laboratory model to study these planetary waves—a crude affair consisting of a rotating dishpan filled with water, and heated at the rim and cooled at the center. This is an analog of the atmosphere viewed from a vantage point high above the pole. The tempest in a dishpan produced rippling wavelike currents in the water similar to planetary waves in the atmosphere, and also high-speed currents something like the jet streams.

Among the early users of numerical weather-prediction techniques was Jerome Namias. Namias originally worked with Professor Rossby at the Massachusetts Institute of Technology, but transferred with the project to the U.S. Weather Bureau in 1940. Numerical predictions were based on the belief that planetary waves father most of the weather in northern latitudes. Numerical predictions were made for the movement of the planetary waves, and 5- and 30-day predictions were made available some years ago from the Weather Bureau on a subscription basis. The 30-day series cost only $4.80 per year, incidentally.

The computer has proved that it can prepare 24- and 48-hour numerical weather predictions in far less time, and more accurately than can human weathermen. This has been demonstrated by comparing human and computer predictions with the actual weather conditions that come about at the time for which the forecast is made. In 1966, for example, the Central Forecasting Office in England switched from hand-drawn charts to computer projections. A 48-hour prediction requires about 1¼ hours to prepare.

Increasing the accuracy of numerical weather prediction makes great demands on a computer, since it requires the processing of many pieces of information, plus immediate solutions. The British Meteorological Office in 1966 was begging the computer industry to provide it with much faster computers. An improved mathematical model of the atmosphere makes it possible to predict when it will rain, with an accuracy of less than an hour; and where it will rain, to closer than 20 miles. Unfortunately, the computer available requires 8 hours to perform the computations for this very precise prediction feat. By the time the results are distributed they are not nearly as useful. And it is pointed out that 8 hours of high-priced computer time per day puts a strain on the budget.

What the British want is a machine capable of doing the analysis and prediction in 20 minutes, but they must wait until about 1970 for such a high-speed computer.

The Great Debate

Numerical weather prediction is based on the principle of determinism, and for this reason some meteorologists and mathematicians believe that it must fail, since man cannot really know enough bits of information to predict accurately a weather future that may stem largely from a tiny, isolated bit of data. Opposing the determinists are the statistical meteorologists.

Dr. Irving Langmuir was persuaded that the determinists were on the wrong track. He said that it might well prove easier to control weather than to predict it; in effect, the only way to predict weather accurately was to make it do what was predicted or desired. Professor C. G. Rossby, whose name was given to the equations he worked out for numerical weather analysis, was among the determinists, although he realistically agreed that if Langmuir were right, the determinists must be wrong and their work would fail. The battle between the deterministic and the statistical approaches hinges then on the idea of the unknowability of the "quantum jump." Physicists cannot predict the motion of these tiniest energy particles, any more than a corps of detectives can predict the erratic act of a madman determined to kill a head of state.

According to Langmuir, there are just too many variables, too many divergent phenomena that can be of great importance. The atmosphere, he said, was too unstable for accurate prediction—and he believed he had proved this with his famous silver-iodide experiment that seemed to cause torrential rains across the whole country every week.

Another man who disagrees with the determinists is Dr. Irving Krick, for 15 years head of the weather department at California Institute of Technology, and advocate of the "Caltech method" of statistical weather prediction. During World War II he used these methods for the Armed Services, and was one of a six-man U.S. Army Air Forces weather board that decided the day of the great invasion of Normandy. Among the most influential of the "industrial weather forecasters," Krick heads Water Resources Corporation, providing weather forecasts and also rainmaking service and hail-suppression for clients for a fee.

An outspoken foe of government weathermen, Krick stanchly defends his "analog" methods and makes predictions of weather years in advance, including weather to be expected for the inauguration of Presidents. His work at the California Institute of Technology included rain predictions for baseball teams interested in buying insurance to protect their gate receipts, and forecasts for Western Air Lines, which was not satisfied with the service provided by the U.S. Weather Bureau.

Armed with daily weather maps dating back to 1899, electronic computers, and a theory that weather is largely influenced by heating in the upper atmosphere and by cyclical waves caused by heating and the tug of sun and moon, Krick "draws a line through past performance and current weather" to predict future weather. It is ridiculous, he says, to try to predict on the basis of present weather only, since it takes two points to determine a line. With only one point as a guide, the weatherman may draw his line anywhere and miss the truth by 180 degrees. Indeed, he points to the fact that many times his forecasts vary that much from those of the government, and are still right. Krick claims that Weather Bureau forecasts of temperature are only 10 per cent more accurate than predicting no change, and precipitation forecasts only 1 per cent better. Krick says he grosses a million dollars a year with his forecasting and rainmaking services and is positive that he and not the numerical-prediction meteorologist is on the right track. One of the biggest complaints of those suspicious of numerical prediction is that the computer men "just don't have enough stuff to crank into their electronic machines."

Krick feels that the analog method by itself is sufficient for predictions a week ahead, but relies on the more complex upper-atmosphere theory for longer forecasts. In his opinion the movement of this atmosphere upward as much as several miles when heated, and its north-and-south movement over the Equator, have a great effect on all the weather taking place below them.

The earth's atmosphere is elastic, he says. Action of the upper atmosphere creates pressure waves that travel systematically. High barometric pressure at the surface indicates that the upper atmosphere is piled high over us in a crest, while low pressure means there is a trough there. He calls this approach to predictions "cosmic meteorology," reminiscent of Aristotle's *Meteorologica,* which treated weather and astronomy within the same covers.

While most of Krick's weather-prediction services are for farmers and industry, some are of a more dramatic nature. For example, he has cited accurate inaugural weather forecasts for Presidents Eisenhower, Kennedy, and Johnson. Krick makes no claim for political-climate prognostications, however.

Looking well ahead, as did the amateur "Sage of Brooklyn"

more than a century ago, Krick forecast suitable weather for the 1966 Titan 1–Gemini 8 launch back in February of 1963, three years ahead of the actual event.

Just how the battle between the determinists and the statisticians will be resolved remains to be seen. The willingness of the two schools of meteorological thought to borrow each other's tools and techniques seems to point to an eventual synthesis of approaches to weather prediction. When man can accurately predict the weather, and if some scientists are right about prediction being at worst impossible and at best more difficult than control of the weather, then we shall obviously be in control of the weather.

4

The History of Rainmaking

THE water crisis is no new problem. The first men needed the liquid just as we do now, although they did not use as many gallons so prodigally as we. Life cannot be sustained without water, and so its importance was recognized before men gave it a name. In some fortunate localities there was a constant supply of running water; in most there was not and early men depended on rainfall for water to drink and to irrigate the crops.

It is easy now for the dullest of us to ridicule the early rainmaking attempts of man but in those prescientific days he was willing to try anything to bring down the rain so needed when sun parched the land for long periods. And we must face the fact that even some of those among us today still cling unconsciously to a few pet superstitions.

For example, when the new moon is tilted, like a bowl spilling water, there will be rainy weather. But when its horns are level none will spill and we will have dry weather.

Often a major duty of a primitive chief was to bring rain for his people. As a hedge against failure, the wise chief delegated a separate rainmaker to do the job. Then if rain did not come, it was the luckless assistant who was punished, rather than the chief himself. After all, the chief had other duties, including finding food, fighting off enemies and wild animals, and so on. Quite early, then, appeared the rainmaker, forerunner of the weather scientist. Here was a man with the time—and the incentive!—to investigate the weather. Here was the first meteorologist, thou-

NASA

A modern weatherman uses a special antenna to track the Tiros weather satellite for reception of cloud-cover photographs.

sands of years removed from his modern-day successors, who would finally bring real weather knowledge to mankind.

It is hard to put ourselves in the place of dawn man. Knowledge once gained is hard to set aside for a fresh look at the world that surrounds us. Today we know where rain comes from and what causes the wind to blow, but the early rainmakers, who were perhaps among the most intelligent primitive men, had to guess at scientific reasons for these phenomena. That their guesses were wide of the mark is understandable. The rainmaker of centuries ago was like a child playing at magic—for all the hope of success he might have. That these gentlemen succeeded in duping their tribes and preserving their own lives is tribute enough to them, not counting the fact that they did set the stage for learned inquiry into causes of weather.

The first painted rainmakers who tried to induce the heavens to part with rain were magicians. A second generation added religion to magic; in time religion would take over as a form of rainmaking in its own right. From these beginnings in due time would come pseudo-scientific attempts, and finally—it is now believed—truly scientific methods of making it rain or not rain, and other modifications of the weather or climate. Mankind has long accorded the rainmaker an important and sometimes honored position.

Magic in Rainmaking

Impossible as it is, let us try to put ourselves in the shoes—or whatever foot coverings were used at the time—of a primitive rainmaker. Our task is readily defined and the rewards even more obvious. If rain comes, we are assured of a pleasant existence. If it does not, we are not assured of any existence at all. We are therefore going to try mightily to make it rain. How shall we do this? A child learns to beckon to another to make him come; children must have done this thousands of years ago. This same sort of imitative gesture was adopted to make it rain. In a kind of "pump priming" aping, the primitive rainmaker often sprinkled water on the soil he wished the heavens themselves to douse.

This imitative, or "homeopathic" magic has an appealing if naïve logic. Some rainmakers hammer on drums to imitate thunder, throw firebrands to simulate lightning, and blow mouthfuls of water into the air like rain or mist. "See," they are saying, "*this* is what we want from you heavens. Come on now,

send us rain!" What more natural method than this? You ask a
man to do something, and is not nature something like a man?

There were—and still are—many variations of homeopathic
weather magic. In some areas women carried water to the fields
at night and poured it out to coax the skies to do the same.
American Indians blew water from special pipes in imitation of
the rainfall. Australian aborigines developed a more complicated
bit of role playing to instruct laggard nature. They built a small
hut of logs and branches and filled it with men of the tribe.
Rainmakers have their arms slit and sprinkle blood on the
assembly. Next, bird down is tossed about in the hut, some of it
clinging to the blood. Here is the symbolizing of rain and clouds.
Two large stones are brought in then, and the rainmakers carry
them from the hut some distance and place them in a tree, since
they too represent clouds. Gypsum, pounded fine, is thrown into
the hole beneath the hut, and finally the men of the tribe leave
the hut and batter it apart with their heads! This last act
symbolizes the penetration of a cloud, and the fall of rain.

Taking baths, throwing people into the river, and even "plow-
ing" the rain by teams of girls who haul a plow through the
river—all were resorted to, to make rain. Another form of
imitation was the use of the frog to bring rain. Because many
frogs are seen following rain, it was believed (and still is by
some) that frogs came down in the rain. Frogs were hung from
trees so that the heavens would pour down rain upon them.

When imitation failed, the rainmaker often resorted to supplication. Children were sometimes buried up to their necks in the
parched ground, and then cried for rain, their tears adding the
imitative magic of other attempts. When even supplication could
not wring tears of compassion from the selfish clouds, a rainmaker might resort to intimidation. "Rain, or I shall injure
you!" was the cry, as he rushed about flailing at the sky with stick
or sword or whip.

At times, rainmakers have been so spectacularly successful that
floods have carried them and their people off. So the magician
must be able to stop the rain, too. Again, imitative magic was
called upon and reverse procedure used. Instead of sprinkling

water or blood about, the rainmaker, or "rainceaser" as he now considers himself, flings torches at the sky or puts out hot rocks to dry up the rain. Baths are not taken. Sometimes naked youngsters are sent out into the rain with a torch to induce the sky to stop the downpour.

Another bit of imitative magic was to face a black horse toward the wind and rub his back with a black cloth. Here the horse signified a cloud, as if somehow this treatment would coax the real black cloud to give up its rain.

Control of Sun and Wind

As rain was vital to life, so too was the sun, and early magicians concerned with weather sometimes tried to control the sun. When an eclipse blotted out the great light, fire-tipped arrows were hastily shot into the air in desperate attempts to relight it. Other magic included burying brands beneath the earth so that they would not be extinguished also, and lighting brands and holding them skyward as a model for the "dead" sun.

Some Indian tribes put on traveling robes, carried walking sticks, and walked in a circle as if heavily laden during an eclipse to help support the tottering sun. In Egypt similar magic assured the continuance of the sun in its path across the sky. Just as there were rainstones to promote precipitation, there were disk-shaped stones drilled with holes and used to cause the sun to shine brightly and eat up the clouds.

Attempts to stay the sun have been numerous and persist in legends and even in games. Peruvians strung a net between two towers to catch the sun. The Eskimo cat's cradle network of string tries to stay the sun from leaving during the Arctic night. And the Eskimo cup-and-ball toy was once a method of pulling the sun back from that darkness! Australian bushmen thought they could delay the sun by putting a clod of dirt in the fork of a tree at just the height of the sun, or hasten its departure by blowing sand after it.

Today man seeks to tame the furious wind of tornadoes and

hurricanes. Early weather wizards had the same thought in mind, though not the scientific approach to the job. Even winds of less than storm intensity can be important, and primitive peoples have long used such things as wind stones to conjure up refreshing breezes on hot days. The Jakuts, for example, favored a stone found in an animal or fish. Wrapped with horsehair, and tied to a stick, this talisman was waved to bring welcome wind. Hottentots believed they could make the wind stop by hanging up a large animal skin, which would simply bar the wind's progress.

Scottish witches conjured up the wind by beating a stone three times with a rag dipped in water, intoning like characters in a Shakespearean play:

> I knok this rag upone this stone
> To raise the wind in the divellis name,
> It sall not lye till I please againe.

New Guinea natives used wind stones upon which they tapped with a stick, and the force of the blow brought anything from a zephyr to a hurricane. Some of the New Guinea tribes claimed to cause wind simply by blowing with their mouths. And pregnant women in Greenland were thought to be able simply to go outdoors, take a breath, and exhale it indoors to calm a storm.

Even as modern-day weather makers, these early magicians ran into all sorts of legal problems. For example, Sopater, a weather maker to Constantine, was accused of tying up the winds so that grain ships from Egypt and Syria were unable to reach Constantinople. Poor Sopater paid with his life for his faulty wind making.

In Scandinavian countries, where wind was important to seafaring men, witches sold knotted bits of string and cloth, which contained the wind. Untying one knot produced a moderate wind; two a gale, and three a violent storm. In this century, Shetland sailors still bought witches' handkerchiefs knotted thrice and containing the wind. There is ancient tradition for such wind control, since Ulysses himself carried a leather bag of wind given him by Aeolus, god of winds.

The weather magician has also used the intimidation technique on the winds, as he did with rain. Herodotus describes a great Sahara Desert wind that had dried up all the water tanks in Tripoli. Angered, a band of people marched out to battle with the south wind, only to perish to a man when a howling simoon wind buried them with sand.

RELIGIOUS RAINMAKING

Somewhere in prehistory, the rainmakers turned from magic to gods. Imitative magic gave way to supplication. The sympathy approach had been used before; now it was directed not to the clouds themselves, or the heavens, but to gods of those various phenomena. Once the tribal chiefs or the appointed rainmakers themselves were thought to be the source of the rain. Slowly that respect shifted. First, perhaps, it was given to the dead. Many old rituals involved supplication at the tomb of a departed ancestor, the dripping of water on his grave, or even the disinterment and reburial of the bones to foster rain or dry weather.

"Praying for rain" is an idea firmly rooted in our culture and the language itself. Men prayed for rain to the dead, and then to gods. Some men still do so, just as some still stage rain dances that are combined magico-religious rites. The rain god was an important figure, and Jupiter Pluvius reigned among the supreme.

The prayer itself might bring rain, but as insurance the idea of rendering gifts or payment to the rain gods grew. At first these sacrificial gifts might have been inanimate objects, but, just as the sun worshipers traded lives for the life the sun gave, rainmakers came to sacrifice living things in exchange for rain. Frogs and other animals at first, and then living human sacrifices. Once the chief or his rainmaker had been slain for failing to bring rain; now a substitute was found by the chief or wizard to save their own lives. Often the sacrifice was a captured enemy. North American Indians, for example, roasted young women from enemy tribes over a slow fire, and then killed them with arrows before eating their hearts and burying the rest in the fields they wanted irrigated with rainfall. Lucky the humans in an area where such lesser sacrifices as a jug of beer were made to the Bringer of Rain!

The Greek Zeus was imagined to make rain by pouring water on earth through a sieve. When prayers and demonstrations failed in ancient Greece, the priest of Zeus climbed Mount Lycaeus to a certain spring and dipped an oak branch into it. This was thought to send up a misty cloud and to bring on rain over the land.

In China huge paper dragons were part of religious festivals to bring rain. If drought prevailed, the dragon was angrily torn to bits. In other religions priests have been dumped into the water and threatened with physical violence if the rains did not come. One technique was to uproot statues and stand them on their heads, or do the same to small figures of the saints, until rainy weather arrived. As late as 1893, Italians suffering from a long drought "banished" the statues of the saints. At Palermo, St. Joseph himself was thrown irreverently into a garden so that he could see how bad things were. Other statues were turned to the wall for shame. One patron saint was stripped of his wings and another put in irons and threatened with hanging if it did not rain!

Understandably, the cross was considered a strong talisman for use in changing the weather. So was the church bell, and Schiller's poem "The Bell" describes the inscriptions on old bells that "called the live, mourned the dead, and brought the lightning." Among the attempts at changing the weather was the erection of crosses and bells to protect the vineyards so important to the economy. The bells, particularly, were thought to prevent hail, lightning, and windstorms, and some are still rung loudly today for this purpose.

It is undeniable that sometimes when we pray for rain we get rain, and that Indian dancers have been drenched before they completed their ritualistic steps. The beaters on rain stones produced results part of the time, and many animal and human sacrifices seemingly did not die in vain when the heavens opened up in repayment for the gift. Also undeniable is the fact that the rainmakers often failed in their task. But faced with drought and death from thirst, it would take a special kind of fool to do absolutely nothing at all. Sooner or later rain came, and who knew but what the gods that controlled them were merely tardy or whimsical? So down through the ages before man made records, and for all the time since, rainmakers of one sort or another have plied their trade of enticing precipitation from the reluctant skies. As noted earlier, the most primitive and unscientific practitioner was nevertheless the father of weather science as we know it today, even though the ultimate of that science may yet be as far removed from us as we are from the jungle rainmaker exhorting his god.

Somewhere along the way the first real step from magic to science was taken when a rainmaker observed a natural truth, perhaps such as the fact that rainy weather followed cold, or that a volcanic eruption triggered rain and that a great fire might do the same thing. Long ago one of the rites in stopping rain was the blowing of a handful of lime, and although this tiny amount of drying agent was completely ineffectual, there was a basic scientific logic behind it. So magic gave way to scientific inquiry.

Pseudo-Science in Rainmaking

Along with using their puny swords, ancient weathermakers occasionally fired a cannon at the wind to still it. The intent seems to have been to treat the wind as any other enemy, and blast it out of existence by sheer force. But perhaps the weatherman was remembering the age-old legends concerning battlefields and rain. Plutarch, writing some two thousand years ago, pointed out that it had been observed that large battles were generally followed by rain. This was long before the days of cannon, and it is interesting to learn what the connection was between the fighting and the rain that followed. One early explanation was religious, and stated that the gods were offended by the carnage, and sent the rains to purge the blood and gore that mortals made. But materialists had another answer: rain was simply the condensation of the blood, sweat, and tears of the warriors as they slaughtered each other on the plains of battle.

Here was a theory far removed from such notions as Zeus pouring water from heaven through a sieve, or some other god drenching the earth because a pet frog's pond was drying up. At least the idea of the evaporation of liquid from the earth, and its subsequent condensation, stood the test of known science. But alas the quantities involved break down the blood-sweat-rain theory. As a later and more scientific observer pointed out, even if 10,000 men were all liquid and all of them were completely vaporized and later condensed as rain, the result would be only about half an inch of rain on a small field.

There were other theories than the vaporization-condensation of body liquids. Noise might cause the rain—indeed, didn't the pealing of bells cause or prevent rain and other weather phenomena? There was much shouting and tumult in battle; the clash of swords and shields as well as the cries and screams that attended the fighting. And what of the dust itself? And the heat of battle. Later, as gunpowder joined the fray, the battle-rain proponents picked up another strong argument. Here was even louder noise, heat, and particles of foreign matter. Surely there must be scientific connection between war and rain! For example, the memoirs of Benvenuto Cellini mention that an impending rainstorm was averted in the year 1539 on the occasion of a procession in Rome, by his firing of artillery in the direction of the clouds, "which had already begun to drop their moisture."

Science demolished the argument, however. Battles are generally fought in areas of rainfall, because other areas are not worth fighting over. Battles are also fought generally in good weather. Thus, by the time a battle is ended, it is about time for rain to fall, and it generally does. Even without the battle, and the assortment of catalysts suspected—the noise and dust and heat and powder—the rains would have come anyway. But at least these were halfway sensible arguments in seeking out the cause of rain, and legends die hard.

The tenders of grapes had long relied on church bells to ward off hail that damaged their fruit. Now with cannon available, some with a more scientific turn of mind began to experiment with the noisemakers. Before we smile in a superior way, remember that this was only the dawn of the scientific revolution and it was excusable that such simple cause-and-effect schemes be tried. It was observable that rain sometimes followed the flash of lightning and the peal of thunder, although the different speeds of those three phenomena had the effect of reversing the actual order. Rain might well be inducing the lightning and thunder, instead of vice versa.

Be that as it may, here was the old idea of imitative magic put to at least pseudo-scientific use. If nature made rain with a flash and a roar, man might do the same. So cannon fired flame and smoke and noise into incipient rain clouds. Sometimes the rain came, and then the rainmakers exulted loudly and took credit. An American argument in favor of the noise-and-smoke theory was that the Fourth of July was often a wet time of year, and what more natural to think than that it was the fireworks that did it! We will see that one of the most modern methods of altering weather is the firing of rockets into the sky, but the old Fourth-of-July hypothesis doesn't stand up under a true scientific test. Weather records covering periods of as long as several decades show that during the time this country celebrated noisily and smokily, there was not any more rain on the average than when we shifted to safe and sane celebrating.

To those who persisted with the argument that violent sound could produce the great gushes of rain sometimes noted during a thunderstorm, the scientist came back with the explanation that the loudest level of audible sound changed the pressure of the air locally only about 1/1000 from normal, hardly enough to cause any wringing of moisture from it. (Today even the scientist is beginning to think lightning may be a factor in rain gushes.)

Explosions held sway for some time. In 1880 U.S. Patent No. 230,067 was issued to Daniel Ruggles for a scheme using a balloon loaded with explosives. By 1891 explosives had gained enough popularity as a rainmaker that the Congress of the United States appropriated the then goodly sum of $9,000 for experiments under control of the Department of Agriculture. Preliminary tests were conducted in Washington, D.C., and then

General Robert Dyrenforth went to Texas and carried out the rainmaking proper. Dyrenforth used dynamite and also hydrogen-oxygen balloons. Some rain actually fell, and there was great rejoicing until it was learned that it had already been predicted by old-fashioned weathermen. In the tests, San Diego, Texas, received .47 inches of rain from October 4 to November 16. A Weather Bureau official at San Antonio admitted that the explosions probably hastened precipitation.

By 1911 and 1912 C.W. Post, nicknamed Postum Post and still famed today for his cereals, conducted private rainmaking tests with bombs. Rain fell immediately, and Post was sure he had succeeded as an artificial weathermaker until it was learned that it rained that day over much of the country. Of course, his dynamite bombs might have touched off a national rain, but Post could not take that much credit.

CHEMICAL RAINMAKING

We mentioned that powdered lime was blown into the air in rain-stopping rites. It is not surprising that other chemicals were used long years ago in efforts to induce rain. Dr. David Livingstone in the 1800's wrote of Sechale, an African witch doctor who made rain with a smoke of charcoal made of excreta, baboon hearts, bat wings, jackal livers, lion hair, tubers, roots, and bulbs. This concoction was burned beneath clouds and made rain, according to Livingstone.

Until near the turn of the century, the scientific weather making had been about as scientific as the medical remedies bottled under the name and picture of Chief Kickapoo. But now the rainmaker began to go through more than hocus-pocus motions as he tried to coax moisture from passing clouds.

In 1875 the French scientist M. Coulier discovered the presence of contaminant particles in normal atmosphere. By 1879 the meteorologist Aitken measured these "condensation nuclei," particles as small as 0.00001 centimeter in diameter. Today they are called Aitken nuclei. Here at last was a mechanism for the phenomenon of precipitation. In the following years additional nuclei were discovered, including ice crystals, dust, sea-salt crystals, and so forth.

Condensation nuclei are tiny particles on which moisture can

NASA

Tiros weather satellite orbiting over global weather.

collect or aggregate into a size sufficient to result in a raindrop large enough to join with others and fall. Aha! This was why it sometimes rained during a volcanic eruption, the rainmakers pronounced, and proceeded to go aloft armed with sacks of dust. But, as the scientists later told them, there was already a sufficiency of dust in the air. Adding more of the same only made the air harder to see through and brought no rain at all.

If dust would not work, sulphuric acid or salt might. But they didn't, and posed the threat of corrosion and coating the earth with a sticky mass that would harm vegetation instead of helping it to grow.

In 1903 in Broken Hill, Australia (where rainmaking experiments continue today, since the same problems of drought prevail), zinc bubbled away in pots of sulphuric acid in an attempt to cause rain. The theory was this: The chemical action of the zinc and acid produced hydrogen gas. This gas, being much lighter than air, would rise; in doing so it created upcurrents of air that would carry moisture high enough to condense out as rain. Again, real science broke this claim down for the fallacy it was. Even if a thousand cubic feet of gas could be generated a minute, it would have taken 280 years to make a cubic mile of it! Not considering the amount of money spent on zinc and acid, the long wait alone would be enough to discourage the experimenter.

In 1887 an inventor received a patent on an explosive device for destroying tornadoes. This was to be hung on a pole a mile southwest of the town to be protected. Here was sound and fury signifying very little, but in 1890, Louis Gathmann of Chicago reportedly fired a shell containing carbon dioxide into the air, causing some effect on a cloud. In 1891 U.S. Patent No. 462,795 was issued to Gathmann for creating rain by releasing liquid carbon dioxide in the upper atmosphere by means of an exploding balloon. This rainmaking technique and material was half a century ahead of its time, but like many such advanced ideas, nothing came of it. Rainmakers returned to less exotic methods and chemicals.

One of the most famous rainmakers of all time was Charles Warren Hatfield who roamed the country for a decade earning fabulous fees for bringing rain to parched regions. Hatfield's equipment consisted of a platform 25 feet high from which a secret device fumed chemicals that he claimed created rain.

Carried on the wind for distances of many miles, the chemicals allegedly caused rain great distances from where they were introduced, and sometimes brought downpours to those who had not paid a fee for his services.

Not always was Hatfield successful, of course, but on one occasion it was not a lack of rain, but too much of it that was his downfall. In January, 1916, Hatfield signed a contract with the city council in San Diego, California, where no rain had fallen for a long time. For each inch of precipitation the rainmaker produced he was to be paid $1,000. After Hatfield had fired up his apparatus, a whopping 20 inches of rain fell in the back country and demolished Lower Otay Dam! The resulting flood killed seventeen people and did millions of dollars damage. The panicky city fathers offered Hatfield a choice of assuming financial responsibility for the inevitable lawsuits, or fleeing town with no pay, and he wisely chose the latter course.

Fair or not, the rainmaker received nothing for his services, and was perhaps lucky to leave the vicinity with skin intact. But there are those today who look back at the occurrence and wryly suggest that there is a Pied Piper aspect to the cheating of the rainmakers, since there is seldom a good rain in the area. The deluge did not curb Hatfield's rainmaking efforts, and in the 1920's he was still asking and getting up to $4,000 for one inch of rain.

The financial success of the rainmakers was evident in the contracts given to Dr. G. A. I. M. Sykes to prevent rain at the Westchester Racing Association meet in 1929. Sykes got $1,000 a day for a week. He also made money by creating rain on demand, or at least getting credit for the precipitation.

SCIENTIFIC RAINMAKING

As early as 1830, meteorologist James Pollard Espy had described the convection currents necessary to form clouds. Rising air was cooled, and as it cooled the moisture in it condensed. The clouds formed were necessary if it was to rain. Would-be rainmakers forthwith concentrated on methods for forcing air to rise. One patented scheme involved a large metal tube, some 1,500 feet high, through which air was to be blown. The beauty of this scheme was that reversing the process would clear away rain! Just how such a monstrous chimney would be fabricated and erected, to say nothing of the problem of withstanding the wind, was not properly spelled out, and nothing came of the ambitious project.

There was, of course, a simpler way of making air rise to great heights. It had been guessed long ago that great natural fires might cause rain, and in 1784 a Jesuit missionary in South America reported seeing Indians burn grass deliberately to make a cooling rain. In the United States a Virginian reported (earlier than 1839) the following occurrence; quoted in *The American Meteorological Journal:**

In the month of August, after a long dry season, it was proposed to set fire to the clearing (10 acres of dry brush), the day was clear; not a cloud to be seen, and was selected for its calmness for fear the fire would damage other property. Well, all hands were called, fire obtained, many of us went to work, the leaves were so dry the brush ignited with great rapidity; in a few moments the whole circle of the clearing was on fire; very soon a strong wind set in from all points on the compass; the smoke and flames assumed an upward gyral motion (like a whirlwind) a cloud was soon formed and a fine rain fell for miles around. I was convinced that the rain was produced by that fire.

In 1839 Espy proposed making rain with fire. He pointed out that only three things could prevent rain from falling under such conditions: a high-altitude current of air that would blow away the heated rising air; a high stratum of air that the rising column of air could not penetrate sufficiently: and insufficient humidity.

Espy declared that if Congress would offer sufficient remuneration he would take the risks involved in attempting to make rain with fire. The legislators, however, were not as daring or free with research and development appropriations as a later Con-

---

* Vol. VIII, May, 1891–April, 1892, p. 484.

gress that underwrote the explosion experiments in rainmaking. Surveyors in Florida reportedly burned sawgrass in large parcels and caused rain, and the Chicago fire in 1871 was followed by rain some said was caused by the fire. But rainmaking with fire was doomed from the start, according to other meteorologists than Espy.

Hot air rises, and nature uses this means to produce the puffy cumulus clouds familiar to everyone, and great producers of rain under the right circumstances. The sun generally furnished the heat required, but a great fire could do the same thing, as had been occasionally observed. Why not touch off fires intentionally, or burn great quantities of fuel in burners located strategically in drought areas? Again, the problem was one of economics. To produce half an inch of rain over a square mile would require the burning of 6,400 tons of coal, or more than a million gallons of oil. To yield a half-inch of rain over a 60-square-mile area would require 75-million-horsepower hours. It was becoming apparent just how much energy was involved in nature's rainmaking process, and the prospect of expending all available fuel to produce rain led the rainmakers to consider other methods of artificially inducing rain.

Orographic Lifting

Nature lifts air in another way than by vertical currents. When wind blows horizontally across a mountain, the air is forced up to higher altitudes like a vehicle going up a hill. In areas where there was a shortage of rain, it was suggested, why not build such a ramp extending a mile high and a hundred miles long? Such a rain catcher should indeed produce "orographic" rainfall when suitable clouds and winds prevailed. But to throw up such a rampart would require an estimated 50 billion freight carloads of rock or dirt! There was another problem to be faced too. The artificial ramp would rob the area downwind of the rain it should have got, and quite likely result in no net gain in rainfall.

U.S. Department of Commerce, Weather Bureau

A meteorologist at the console of the IBM 7090 electronic computer in the Joint Numerical Weather Prediction Unit of the U.S. Weather Bureau's National Meteorological Center at Suitland, Maryland. The high-speed computer processes weather data for short- and long-range forecasts and analyses, and for research.

PUTTING THE AIRPLANE TO WORK

Other, simpler means for forcing air upward were suggested. One of these was to tie down a number of surplus airplanes (this was after World War I) with their tails pointing toward a common center point. When all the engines were started, the propellers would blow air in toward the center, and it would have to rise in a great column that would eventually reach high altitudes and produce clouds.

U.S. *Department of Commerce, Weather Bureau*

Carl Gustav Rossby, the weather scientist who figured prominently in numerical prediction.

Proponents of these and other schemes for mechanically lifting great volumes of air were doomed to failure on engineering and economical grounds. Even if there were enough aircraft available to create rain over a large area, the fuel for running the engines would cost more than that which could transport water in tank cars a distance of a thousand miles or more. So the idea of colossal metal tubes poking into the sky or of surplus fighter planes tethered in a ring like pawing oxen proved more interesting in Sunday supplements than on engineering drawing boards.

CHILLING THE AIR

Moisture condenses out of rising air because of the cooling that takes place as altitude is gained. Some inventive genius wondered why not simply cool the air right at ground level. Such a thought was obviously inspired by watching the pitcher of ice water "sweat" on the dining room table on a warm and humid day. Again, the physicist shot holes in this bold plan: refrigeration to squeeze the water out of the air would increase the price of such water to about 10,000 times what the farmer was then paying for his irrigation. And such a system obviously could only work in warm, humid weather. Droughts usually involve hot, dry weather.

The airplane had been suggested as a rainmaking device, but in a rather crude and ignoble form with its wings removed and its tail anchored to the ground. Why not use the craft in its true element, high above the ground and right in nature's weather factory? Early experiments had involved exploding bombs in balloons; now the rainmakers climbed into aircraft and took themselves and their apparatus up into the clouds.

If cooling the air was the answer, some were determined to sow ice from a speeding plane and reap a downpour as the air cooled and formed a rain cloud. An improvement on this idea was the use of carbon dioxide, and here the rainmaker was coming tantalizingly close to success, even though the scientist pointed out to him that he was still barking up the wrong cloud.

As one meteorologist put it, "This method has been tried. It didn't work, and it never will, for it is wrong even in principle." He then proceeded to demolish the scheme on the grounds that simply cooling the air could not do the job. But at last the pluviologist had caught up with his science-rooted detractors. Wrong as it might have been in principle, carbon dioxide, or dry ice, could indeed cause rain to fall, as Vincent Schaefer would prove later!

The rainmaking experimenter was often woefully short on real scientific knowledge. But often too the scientist was guilty of having his blinders of truth on a bit too tight. All that was needed now to cause rain was to try seeding clouds with dry ice to create *freezing nuclei,* rather than to use it as a cooling agent. Unfortunately, this was not done for some time. Many other kinds of seeding, or dusting as it was once called, were tried, however.

ELECTRICAL RAINMAKING

The advent of electricity touched off schemes to do everything from rejuvenating tired humans to causing rain to fall. Lightning is involved in thunderstorms, thus testifying to the presence of electricity as part of the phenomenon. Bare wires were charged with current, and thousands of lightning rods were sold with the advertisement that they would help to bring rain. So sure was the general public that electrical waves were tampering with nature's workings that injunctions were sought against radio stations thought to be causing everything from droughts to floods. But in the early days of electrical rainmaking, no provable results came from the experiments.

Clever rainmakers suggested combining two ideas in one: the dusting of clouds with electrified sand. Here physicists had to agree that the electrical phenomenon was being exploited in a way that might conceivably cause the condensation of water drops about the charged sand particle. The physicists also felt that great quantities of sand would be required to bring appreciable rain.

The best method for using the airplane to bring rain to the parched land below seemed to be to fill the plane with water and spray it in flight. But here again economics defeated the idea. So much water would evaporate in descending that it would require more than 100 tons to provide an inch of rain on just one acre, and air-freighting 100 tons would cost a pretty penny.

CLEARING AWAY THE CLOUDS

The magician of old had a talisman in the form of a stone that could make the sun "eat up the clouds." The pseudo-scientist of the early twentieth century was still trying to find ways to dissipate clouds and prevent rain. Instead of a sun stone, or a cannon or brandished sword, however, he relied on more modern methods ranging from oil burners to aircraft.

Meteorologists noticed that sometimes when a kite was flown just above a thin stratus cloud a wake of clear air would be produced—not because the kite bore a magic inscription and the picture of a dragon, or because of electrification of the kite string, but because air pressure beneath the kite pressed part of the cloud down to a lower level and the moisture warmed and evaporated. It was suggested that an airplane would have even more effect. (Interestingly, one of the fog-chasing methods currently being tried is that of flying a helicopter above the low-hanging cloud.)

Scientists were not hopeful that man with the puny energy at his command could stop a real rainstorm, but clouds could be dissipated in a variety of ways. One would be to fly a plane through a small cloud and disperse it by the blast of the propeller. Another would be to seed the cloud with electrified sand or perhaps liquid air to cool it and cause it to descend. Thus the rainmaker's dream could succeed in just the reverse application he had planned for it!

If the airplane was becoming a tool for use by the rainmaker, it was also creating new applications for him to work on. Fog at airports seriously limited operations and posed a great danger for take off and landing. Here was a small area of need where some of the earlier and impractical ideas might be put to use—not to make it rain but to *clear* the air of moisture.

Electrified sand was suggested, as it had been for rainmaking, but this would involve the dropping of many tons of sand and necessitate an airplane flying in hazardous conditions. But heating the air could easily dissipate the fog. One study in the early 1920's showed that an airport or "aerodrome" as it was then called, could be kept fog-free by burning 6,600 gallons of oil or 35 tons of coal an hour. The obvious drawback was the resultant cost of $330 per hour to keep the field open, assuming a 5-cent-per-gallon cost for oil. However, a single airliner, even in those early days, cost far more than this. And to put a price on a single human life is undesirable if not impossible. So here was a potential application of the rainmaker's magic in our modern world.

Another clever suggestion for clearing fogs was to drain them away through underground pipes. Here air pumps would exhaust the moisture-filled air. But the cost would be high, with more than 100,000 horsepower required to operate the ventilating system, and more fog could keep drifting in. The drainage idea, brilliant as it may have been, was not put to use.

The rainmaker-turned-pseudo-scientist continued to try to stop hailstorms. Cannons were fired, and Ben Franklin's lightning rods were put to use to "draw the teeth" of the lightning and thus prevent hail. Again scientists pooh-poohed the ideas, pointing out that the cannon was far too puny to be of any effect whatsoever on even a moderate electricity to prevent lightning.

Hardly daunted, the rainmaker described plans for taming the lightning with his all-purpose electrified sand, a project which if successful would seem to pose a threat to beaches! Lightning causes countless forest and other fires, and preventing these would be a great blessing from the artificial weather maker or preventer. But scientists scoffed at the notion, one called it "as silly as futile, and as futile as silly."

In answer to the suggestion that sand might be dropped on thunderstorms to curb lightning, meteorologist Humphreys pointed out that his calculations showed that it might take 15,000 pounds of sand to soak up the electric charge in a single bolt of lightning! Tolerating the flashes might be safer than burying an area in sand.

Little precipitation resulted from the rainmakers' efforts, but

U.S. Department of Commerce, Weather Bureau

Jerome Namias, who pioneered Weather Bureau 30-day predictions.

the efforts themselves continued and even increased as the age-old dream kept plaguing the imaginative and persistent minds of men.

Russia created its Turkmenistan Institute of Rainfall in 1930, and experimented with the artificial creation of mists by burning cheap fuel on the ground. Soviet scientists also succeeded in making rain fall from natural clouds. The two ideas were combined and it was announced that the goal of the Institute was to create rainfall artificially even in cloudless areas. Also in 1930 Chinese army airplanes were used to drop a cooling agent called deolin into clouds over Hong Kong, which was suffering a crippling drought. The rainmaking attempt was not successful, however.

One grandiose dream in the United States for wringing moisture out of the reluctant skies was to build a giant "fog screen." One hundred and fifty feet high, and miles long, this strategically placed sieve would condense out the water to be used for irrigation or other purposes. But cost, strength considerations, and other factors kept such a device from being built.

Rain was not all that the weather makers would change. The Weather Bureau was plagued with demands for great coils of wire to be set up around New York City from Atlantic City to Connecticut, to keep the population warm. Westerners, too, had similar ideas and suggested a line of wood-burning stoves from the Red River to the Continental Divide.

The term "pluviculture" was coined in a debunking article in *Nature* magazine in 1921, wherein the author lumped rain-making along with "chiropractic and hormonism." He also suggested a method of protecting the rainmaker with insurance from Lloyd's of London and showed how he could make a tidy profit, rain *or* shine!

War continued between established meteorological institutions and those free-lance weathermen who insisted they could change the weather. By 1930 there was beginning to be a change in the conflict, however: The pluviologist was not nearly as unscientific as he once had been. And he, along with the "legitimate" meteorologist, was about to take the giant step to real rain-making.

"Every cloud has a silver lining."

—Anonymous

5

Modern Rainmaking

It is difficult to pinpoint a time that distinctly marks the change from witch-doctor rainmaking to scientific weather modification but 1930 may well be the pivotal year. It was then that three Europeans were experimenting to find the real causes of precipitation.

August Veraart of Holland went aloft one day in a small plane and seeded clouds with dry ice. Experimenters before him had already dumped a variety of chemicals and other materials into the sky, but Veraart seems the first cloud seeder who really made it rain. This was sixteen years before the feat generally conceded to be the beginning of modern rainmaking, and it was no fault of Veraart's that his name has been pretty much forgotten in the intervening years. The Dutchman claimed loudly that he was truly a rainmaker; in fact, he seems to have made such sweeping claims that he was relegated to the company of those who muttered voodoo incantations and imitatively flung buckets of water skyward.

More respectful attention was paid to Scandinavian Tor Bergeron and Germany's Walter Findeisen. Like Veraart, these two meteorologists felt that the probable mechanism of precipitation was the freezing of water vapor on ice crystals in clouds, touching off a chain reaction that filled the cloud and led to snow, rain, hail, or sleet, depending on other conditions.

Tor Bergeron discovered one of the two ways in which natural rain occurs. In most clouds the droplets of water are too small to fall. They are about 20 microns in diameter rather than the several hundreds of microns required to make a drop heavy enough to fall as rain. Growing by condensation of more water on the tiny drops proceeds at a very slow rate. However, if ice crystals are formed in the cloud, these grow very rapidly, taking moisture at the expense of the liquid water drops.

The presence of nuclei in the atmosphere varies from a minimum of 100 parts per cubic centimeter in clean marine air to 1,000,000 parts per cubic centimeter in smog. One hundred million water droplets may exist in a cubic meter. Their size is indicated by the maximum weight of water contained in that volume of cloud: only one gram. Five hundred cubic meters of cloud thus contain only a little more than one pound of water.

It was believed that the temperature of clouds from which precipitation fell was between freezing and 20 degrees Centigrade below freezing. Water can be much cooler than freezing and still remain a liquid; in fact, a temperature of minus 50 degrees Centigrade has been recorded for liquid water. So something besides cold is needed to cause the physical change from the liquid to the solid state. Findeisen thought that freezing nuclei must be present to trigger the formation of ice crystals that in turn caused snow or other precipitation. Just what these nuclei consisted of he was not sure, but nature must provide them. Furthermore, Findeisen thought man could introduce *artificial* nuclei and so cause precipitation.

He suggested that quartz crystals might serve, since they are hexagonal like ice crystals. He also published some very optimistic predictions on weather modification:

. . . It can be boldly stated that, at comparatively slight expense, it will, in time, be possible to bring about rain artificially, obviate the danger of icing, and prevent the formation of hailstorms. As a result of the accompanying energy transformations, it should also be possible to influence, within limits, other weather phenomena (e.g., temperature, wind) which can probably never be appreciably changed by direct technical means. . . .

As Findeisen was getting warmed up to his work the Nazis plunged Europe into World War II. Since weather is such a potent factor in the pursuit of war, it is understandable that the German government employed Findeisen to continue his weather-modification research. He did not come up with anything of value, however, and his reports were so mediocre and innocuous in fact, that Irving Langmuir suggested Findeisen had purposely withheld more important information. Findeisen was later reported working in Russia.

World War II produced only one weather-modification break-through, if it can be called that. The idea of dissipating fog with heat was an old one; war made it important enough that the British burn as much as 6,000 gallons of fuel to melt away fog for one aircraft to land. This brute-force method was of course too expensive for commercial application in its early form, although we shall see that others are continuing dispersal research with improved thermal devices.

In 1945, however, British scientist Bohdan Cwilong did dis-cover how to cause the spontaneous formation of ice crystals in humid air. Investigating conditions in the stratosphere, he repro-duced them in the laboratory by chilling wet air to minus 35 degrees Centigrade at which point ice crystals suddenly formed. Here was a brute-force method at the other end of the tempera-ture scale. Findeisen had searched for a sublimation nuclei to produce ice crystals, but Cwilong discovered that if one simply cooled the air sufficiently the crystals were bound to form, nuclei or not. Here was a laboratory demonstration to bear out the claims of Veraart some fifteen years earlier, but apparently no one put these separate occurrences together to come up with a workable rainmaking scheme. That would come shortly as a result of independent research in America.

GENERAL ELECTRIC'S ICE MAKERS

Dr. Irving Langmuir won the Nobel Prize in chemistry in 1932, partly for his work with monomolecular films floating on water. Today such films are being used experimentally in weather modification of a sort, by suppressing evaporation from small bodies of water and thus saving the liquid in reservoirs. But World War II carried the eminent scientist into more direct weather applications. In 1942 his work with smoke generators for the Army interested him in fog and its behavior. One result was a theory concerning the growth of water droplets in a cloud. This theory stood the test when Langmuir went to frigid Mount Washington in New Hampshire to research such things as icing conditions on aircraft. His assistant was a young man named Vincent Schaefer, long interested in snow, and inventor of a method of treating flakes to preserve their shapes for photography.

At Mount Washington the two men were impressed by the supercooled clouds that blew over the mountain, clouds that could suddenly and mysteriously turn into snowstorms. Like Bergeron and Findeisen before them, they began to ponder the question of the ice-making "trigger." However, the answer did not come on the icy slopes of Mount Washington, but in a home freezer at the General Electric plant in Schenectady.

Schaefer had begun his work for the firm as a laboratory technician, since his education stopped with high school. But it was soon apparent that his abilities ran far beyond conceiving and building equipment as effective as it was economical. His ice-crystal laboratory setup was typical. Schaefer lined the box with black velvet and mounted a light to illuminate any ice crystals that happened to form in the box. He had the environment now, and thought all he need do was to breathe into the freezer and watch ice crystals form. Strangely, all his puffing produced no crystals, although there was plenty of normal atmospheric dust in the freezer.

Even with the temperature cooled down to minus 23 degrees Centigrade, nothing happened, so Schaefer began dropping possible sublimation nuclei into the box. Some theorists said that volcanic dust was nature's trigger; he tossed in some. Sand had been tried by aerial cloud seeders, but it didn't work in the freezer either. Neither did quartz, as Findeisen had hoped, or such varied substances as diatomaceous earth (which Alfred

Nobel had used by accident to produce dynamite), sulfur, graphite, carbon, or talc. After exhausting logical possibilities including salt, which is present in the atmosphere naturally, he tried long shots like soap powders and sugar. But the little clouds of vapor refused to turn to ice crystals.

Ice crystal. This delicate geometric shape acts as a nucleus for a water drop.

On July 12, 1946, Schaefer went to lunch, leaving the freezer lid open as he usually did, since cold air would not escape from the box. When he returned, the temperature had climbed somewhat higher than he wanted it. The handiest way to cool it down again was to put in some dry ice, which has a temperature of about minus 78 degrees Centigrade. As he bent over the box he exhaled—and lo, there were the long-sought ice crystals! Not just one or a handful in his beam of light, but millions of them. Slowly they formed small snowflakes and the miniature snow-storm settled to the bottom of the freezer.

Schaefer had stumbled onto something by "serendipity," the happy accidental discovery of one thing while seeking something else. He realized that he had not introduced nuclei, but that the low temperature itself had forced sublimation of the supercooled moisture from his breath. Here was spontaneous ice-crystal for-mation like that encountered by Cwilong in Great Britain. To prove that the cold did it, Schaefer chilled a metal rod in liquid air to a temperature of minus 183 degrees Centigrade and used it to produce ice crystals in a cloud of moisture in his freezer box. Further experiments showed that minus 39 degrees Centigrade was the magic temperature for turning supercooled cloud to ice crystals.

Schaefer had made it snow on a hot July day with the help of his deep freeze. On a cold November 13 of that same year he was ready to try the dry-ice treatment on real clouds. For this test he climbed into a small plane with pilot Curtis G. Talbot of General Electric's Flight Test Center. In the floor of the cabin craft was an automatic dispenser for the dry ice to be dropped. The two men took off and began to scout for a likely looking cloud. About 30 miles east of Schenectady, over Greylock Moun-tain in Massachusetts, Schaefer found what he was looking for, a stratus cloud 4 miles long, 14,000 feet high, and cold enough to be supercooled.

The dry-ice dispenser cranked out three of the six pounds of pellets, and then jammed. Cold and fatigued, Schaefer was unable to fix the electric motor that was at fault, so he just dumped the rest of the dry ice out the window. Back at General Electric, Langmuir watched with binoculars, and saw snow fall from the cloud a distance of about 2,000 feet before it evapo-rated. Elated, he met the returning plane and cried to Schaefer "This is history!"

Another watcher had been scanning the skies that day. Young Bernard Vonnegut was interested in the cloud-seeding experiment too, and he picked out a plane he thought was Schaefer's. As he watched, a cloud began to form behind it as if by magic. Then, with chagrin, he realized that the "cloud" was spelling out the name of a soft drink!

Despite the exhausting effects of high-altitude and cold, Schaefer was exhilarated at the results of dumping out dry ice. He wrote that the rapidity with which the dry ice affected the clouds was amazing, and that the cloud seemed to "explode all at once."

For the first time in modern history, man had set out to cause precipitation and succeeded to the satisfaction of the most critical observer. True, the snowfall did not reach the ground, but the experiment was a success. Two similar seeding trials followed, using isolated clouds as targets. Snow fell, but only briefly before melting.

On December 19 the Weather Bureau predicted "fair and warmer" for Schenectady for the following day. On the 20th Schaefer went up again and seeded a cloud 35 miles east of the city. Snow fell for some distance but did not reach the ground. However, a big storm hit Schenectady and dumped 8 inches of snow. Modestly the weather makers disclaimed credit for this one, but felt they could have caused it to start several hours earlier than it did had they seeded early in the day.

When General Electric's legal minds got wind of this possibility they were upset. A General Electric snowstorm could leave the firm wide open to invasion-of-property suits, including hardship and damage. A quick freeze was clamped on the snowmaking experiments, and never again would a General Electric employee seed a cloud. Instead, contracts were negotiated with the U.S. Army Signal Corps, the organization that had pioneered the weather service and also the practical use of airplanes in this country. Soon the Office of Naval Research joined the venture and the resulting weather-modification experiment was called Project Cirrus.

In March, 1947, Captain Clarence Chamberlain, an Air Force pilot participating in Project Cirrus, took a B-25 up through a heavy layer of stratus cloud and his crew seeded a 20-mile path

with 15 pounds of dry ice. Then they circled back to see what
happened. Spectacularly the pellets had carved a vast canyon
through the clouds 5 miles wide and 20 miles long. Chamberlain
said, "Its sides were as sharp and steep as though someone had
taken a spade and shoveled a path through a snowdrift." On the
ground Dr. Langmuir watched snow fall from the seeded area,
while the sky cleared as if by magic.

General Electric

Vincent Schaefer, discoverer of the dry-ice cloud-seeding technique, and
Irving Langmuir, Nobel Prize-winning scientist.

These dramatic successes prompted Langmuir to predict that
planes could be used to clear the skies for air traffic at the rate of
1,000 square miles an hour. Schaefer came up with the idea of
firing carbon dioxide pellets from a gun. He thought it might be
possible to fire them from the nose of a plane flying in clouds and
have them explode two miles ahead, in time to open up a clear
air path for the plane doing the shooting.

Dry ice could make it snow, and also clear clouds from the air.
Within a week of his first cloud-seeding flight, Schaefer had

proved that his cold magic touch could melt away the fog too. When fog blanketed his home, he placed some dry ice in a basket made of screening and whirled it about his head as he walked through the yard. At first the fog became more dense, as the air filled with ice crystals. Then water droplets fed the multiplying crystals and the fog cleared along his path.

Just as dry ice triggered the formation of ice crystals, its success touched off a storm of weather-making interest across the country. Not surprisingly the newspapers were among the first to sponsor weather-making flights. The *Arizona Republic* made rain in July, a first for newspapers, with a two-hour rain over an area of 25 square miles. Hopi Indians in Flagstaff who had recently staged their annual rain dance protested tongue-in-cheek that the white men were not only stealing their thunder, but appropriating their rain clouds as well. The *Chicago Tribune* launched "Operation Mark Twain" and produced rain. And the New York *Herald Tribune* not only claimed success in seeding a cloud, but said it marked a first in artificially breaking a heat wave.

Silver Lining for a Cloud

In all the excitement Schaefer temporarily lost interest in his search for precipitation nuclei. Who needed them, when dry ice worked so well? The stuff cost only a few cents a pound, was readily available, and caused no pollution of the atmosphere as some materials might. Dr. Langmuir calculated that a pellet of dry ice the size of a pea could produce 100,000,000,000,000,000 infinitesimal ice crystals, and that if all these grew to sizable flakes the snowfall would weigh 100,000 tons!

Dr. Bernard Vonnegut, the General Electric scientist who had watched a "cloud" spell out Pepsi-Cola instead of snowfall, kept on with his search for suitable ice nuclei. Findeisen had suggested quartz because of its hexagonal structure, but Vonnegut one day reasoned that the nuclei size factor must be as important as shape. Checking the *Handbook of Chemistry and Physics* he picked out from among 1,300 compounds that of silver iodide.

The "crystal lattice" or atomic structure of the iodide matched that of ice within 1 per cent.

Convinced he was on the right track, Vonnegut obtained a sample of silver iodide and introduced it into the cold box. Not a single crystal resulted! Surprised and disappointed, the young physicist persisted and soon found that the batch of silver iodide was not pure. Another sample was tried, and suddenly there were the beautiful tiny crystals floating in the frigid atmosphere of the freezer, even though the temperature was well above the normal crystallization temperature of minus 39 degrees Centigrade. The effectiveness of the new seeding method was soon demonstrated.

Dry ice at that time cost about a nickel a pound. A pound of pure silver iodide—and it was pointless to use any but pure material, as Vonnegut found—cost $20. Where was the economic justification for using the iodide rather than dry ice, if it cost four hundred times as much? Vonnegut demonstrated by building a "smoke generator" for the stuff that broke an ounce of iodide into 10^{18} particles. One thousand ounces would produce enough particles to put one in each cubic inch of air for a distance of 10 miles above the United States. When Vonnegut burned some silver iodide in the General Electric lab, the smoke drifted 6 miles and started a small snowstorm in a frozen-food cabinet in a grocery store at Alplaus, New York.

On October 14, 1948, Project Cirrus conducted four seedings of clouds near Albuquerque, New Mexico. In the morning, 2 ounces of silver iodide was dispersed from an airplane by dropping it in burning charcoal pellets from an altitude of 12,000 feet. The other three seedings were dry ice, using from 15 to 25 pounds of the material. Dr. Langmuir took credit for producing about 0.35 inch of rain over an area of 4,000 square miles. This was no mean feat, since this much water is about 200 billion gallons.

In July, 1949, experimenters began using silver iodide generators placed on the ground. Here was a tremendous advantage of the iodide method: the particles are small and light enough to be wafted upward on currents of air, whereas dry ice can only fall down through clouds, or be towed in a container back of an airplane. Dr. Langmuir began to use his iodide smoke generator on July 14; on July 21 it operated for 13 hours, commencing at 5:30 in the morning. The results were spectacular to say the least, particularly since the Weather Bureau had predicted no substantial amounts of rain.

General Electric

The results of dry-ice cloud seeding by aircraft during Project Cirrus experiments.

By 8:30 a large cloud began forming about 25 miles south of the generator. The wind was blowing in that direction at about 10 miles an hour, and Langmuir was convinced the iodide seeding was responsible. By 10 o'clock, radar screens showed water droplets in the cloud, lightning commenced, and heavy rainfall began. More thunderclouds formed, and in the afternoon there was 1.2 inches of rain in the area of the smoke generator. Heavy rain also fell in Santa Fe. Within 30 hours of the time, water began to run in normally dry Galisteo Creek, and some 650,000,000 gallons of water flowed through it. Langmuir claimed credit for about 480 billion gallons of rain on New Mexico in two days in 1949.

Langmuir worked out the statistical probability that the rain on October 14, 1948, and July 21, 1959, could have occurred naturally and announced that there was only one chance in 10 million. This claim was met with amazement by most professional meteorologists, one of whom said, "The whole experiment was a great tragedy. If Langmuir actually influenced the weather, no one will believe him. If the periodicity was coincidence, nature played him a dirty trick."

But Langmuir remained firm. It was important now, he said, to conduct further long-range tests on certain days of the week to see if regular effects on the weather would result. On December 6, 1949, he began such a series of tests under Project Cirrus aegis.

Each week Langmuir's lone iodide generator in New Mexico spewed out 700 grams of the seeding material. Invisibly it floated upward and *eastward* on vertical air currents and the prevailing winds. And for the next 140 days the rainfall over more than one million square miles of the United States was from three to ten times as much on Mondays and Tuesdays as it was on Saturdays and Sundays. Langmuir said it was clearly obvious that he had introduced a periodicity in the weather. To make the proof even more convincing, he shifted his day of seeding, and obediently the rainfall east shifted itself to occur on different days of the week.

Not only rainfall, but upper-air temperatures and air pressures also were affected and exhibited the strange weekly period. The changes began about two weeks after Langmuir began to seed the sky; they ceased about two weeks from the time he stopped. For Langmuir this was proof enough that cloud seeding worked. The cost? "Assuming the atmosphere to be 5 miles thick, one thus finds that to get a 30 per cent chance of rain per day within a

given area in New Mexico the cost of the silver iodide is only
$1.00 for 4,000 square miles." Indeed, to double the United States
rainfall, assuming conditions were the same as in New Mexico,
Langmuir felt that it would cost only about $200 a week.

As an example of the "results" of Langmuir's seeding, Buffalo,

U.S. Department of the Interior

A bank of silver-iodide generators used by the Bureau of Reclamation
for cloud seeding. The generators burn silver iodide mixed in acetone
and propane.

New York, got a total of 4.38 inches of rain on twelve consecutive
Tuesdays, and only 0.32 inches on Saturdays. Philadelphia got
2.27 inches on Tuesdays, and 0.19 on Saturdays. Meanwhile,
Texas cattlemen complained that the disastrous drought in the
Southwest was caused by large-scale cloud seeding in the West
and Southwest during the last few years. Langmuir agreed that

this was possible, and that under certain conditions cloud seeding might draw moist Gulf of Mexico air away from Texas to the Mississippi Valley region.

President Eisenhower responded to such complaints by appointing a committee to look into the dangers inherent in weather tampering, such as drought, storms, and flood. On the other side of the coin they were to work toward effective weather control that could bring far-reaching benefits to agriculture, industry, commerce, and the general welfare and common defense. The idea was beginning to dawn that some government regulation of weather making might have to be legislated.

Yet in 1948 and 1949, the Air Force and the Weather Bureau got into the act with a series of cloud-seeding tests independent of Project Cirrus. This experiment was as fruitless as Cirrus was fruitful. It was almost, some suggested, as if the Weather Bureau people had unconsciously slanted their results to bear out a disbelief in the efficacy of cloud seeding.

WARM RAIN

Early scientific rainmakers concentrated on getting rain from supercooled clouds. At the Equator, and in much of the tropics, rain is observed to fall from clouds that are not supercooled, and the mechanism for this precipitation was unknown. In Project Cirrus the experimenters were sometimes surprised to produce rain in clouds that were warmer than those thought susceptible to the seeding process. Who was to knock success? But in 1947 cloud seeders working for pineapple growers in Hawaii reported seeding definitely "warm" clouds and having it rain hard nevertheless. Langmuir had to get busy and find out why.

The "Bergeron process" accounts for rain in supercooled clouds. Another mechanism had to be found to account for rain falling from clouds whose tops do not reach below-freezing temperatures. Nature accomplishes this by creating a few giant droplets in warm clouds. Normally the nuclei present in the atmosphere are about half a micron in diameter. But once in a while there is a salt particle with a diameter as great as 5 microns. Water droplets condensing on these can reach a size of 50 microns rather than the average 20-micron size. Such giant droplets collide with smaller droplets and grow by coalescence, the merging of the two bodies.

Before the month was out Langmuir presented a theory for warm clouds to the National Academy of Sciences. It was most likely not the dry ice, but ordinary ice collected on it that triggered the rain, he told the assembled scientists. In fact, a large enough drop of water should do the trick in a cumulus cloud with plenty of water droplets and a strong updraft blowing in it. The falling drop collects other drops as it falls, but on reaching a certain critical size it breaks into many smaller drops itself, and the chain reaction starts anew.

This new water-seeding process sounded vaguely like the practice of some American Indians of swirling water into the air from their pipes. At any rate, subsequent tests have shown that seeding with water alone can cause rainfall. Another common substance that has been used in tests with warm clouds in India is salt. Some apparent success was achieved, but not enough work was done to prove that it was actually triggered by the rainmakers and not nature.

Meteorologists are continuing to learn about the possible mechanisms of precipitation. For example, it is believed that the proportions of condensation nuclei on a worldwide average basis are:

Combustion products	40%
Soil particles (dust)	20
Sea salt particles	20
Unknown	20

Kaolinite, a form of clay, is a common natural nucleant in tiny dust-particle form. However, there are theories developing on *organic* ice nucleants, including urea, amino acids, terpin hydrates, vanillin, methyl salicylates, eucalyptol and cineole. These are thought to be released by vegetation at rates dependent on the season.

The Amateur Rainmakers

The coming on the rainmaking scene of men such as Irving Langmuir was no guarantee that the old unscientific barnstormer had vanished. Such rainmakers doubled and tripled their numbers with the new and handy mechanism that Schaefer had provided in dry ice. Anybody with a bucket of dry ice and the loan of an airplane could set up shop as a rainmaker. Far too many did just that. Dr. Langmuir noted that some of the results of his carefully controlled New Mexico experiments were "masked" by the results of amateurs doing 50 or 100 times the seeding he did.

Marvelous tales were told of rainmakers bringing down welcome deluges, but for each success is a story of a dozen failures. One cloud seeder made it rain on a neighbor's farm, while his own continued to parch. Another heaved a huge block of dry ice out of a plane into a cloud and on returning found he had smashed a hole through his hangar roof. Overzealous pilots were threatened with lynching for their activities, and suits were filed charging rainmakers with casting a drought "shadow" downwind of their operations.

Some optimists seeded clear blue sky in the vain hope that clouds and rain would follow. Often when clouds were seeded it rained harder in unseeded areas. And sometimes the enthusiasm of the rainmaker resulted in "overseeding" that dried up precipitation as effectively as a sponge. Whether or not such amateur weather modification was a factor in the 5,000 per cent increase in rainfall reported in the Red River Valley in 1950, or how valid were Dr. Langmuir's fears that amateurs had contributed to the floods in the Mississippi Valley, could not be established. But it is probable that for every beneficial rain there were thousands of unproductive hours of flying, and tons of wastefully dropped seeding agents. The only beneficiaries of some unscientific attempts to wring water from the clouds were the purveyors of dry ice.

In the early days of trying to control the weather, rainmakers often did things not based on any formal science. Today, the man who intends to alter the weather had better have some idea what makes it in the first place, and so most rainmakers now are also meteorologists. Dr. Irving Krick is an example. He and most of the rainmakers who brought in the new methods were scientists to begin with, who later became interested in making rain. Following World War II Krick had gone into the private weather forecasting business on a nonprofit basis. With the success of Langmuir and Schaefer, he also began operating a cloud-seeding venture called Water Resources Development Corporation.

Early customers of Krick were the wheat-raising ranchers in the Pacific Northwest. Normal rainfall is about 7.5 inches per year in the area, but each additional inch of rain increased the yield about $3\frac{1}{2}$ bushels per acre. So Krick was asked to try to boost rainfall by 50 per cent. In June of 1950 Krick's smoke generators were credited with increasing rainfall on the fields by almost 2 inches. The resultant increase in the value of the wheat crop was $300,000, some ten times the fee for rainmaking. To determine if Krick got the credit, rainfall on the wheat ranches was compared with that upwind of the iodide smoke "plume." It was found that farmers as far as 60 miles downwind also benefited from the rainmaking.

Another plague of the wheat rancher is hail, and soon Krick was suppressing hail on contract for Canadians. The method used is that of overseeding the clouds. Others using Krick's weather-modification services included a United States government agency, power and utility industries, paper and pulp companies, ski-tow operators, and other interests. Foreign countries also hired Krick and he set up rainmaking systems in France, Spain, Canada, Israel, Africa, Italy, Syria, among others.

Krick's annual rainmaking sales soon jumped to more than one million dollars a year. Costs to clients were about one cent to three cents an acre. In 1952 he began to seed clouds in Spain to increase water for hydroelectric power plants. He also had several hundred silver iodide generators in the western United States. These were turned on at a phone call from Krick by a farmer or perhaps a handy filling-station operator. For the three winters, 1949, 1950 and 1951, his organization claimed credit for increasing the snowpack in the Rockies around Denver 175 per cent to 288 per cent of the previous 10-year average.

According to Krick's figures, his operations increased rainfall from 13 per cent to 15 per cent. A study by the Eisenhower Committee on Weather Control released in 1957 placed the increase in precipitation caused by rainmakers at between 9 per cent and 17 per cent, a close agreement with Krick's estimate.

By 1953 Krick had operated 150 rainmaking projects in 18 states and 6 foreign countries, amassing more than 200,000 hours of seeding time. In December, 1952, Krick's generators (12 of them) began to seed the drainage basin near Dallas, Texas. After six months, involving almost 900 hours of generator operation, water in the basin had increased 363 per cent over the January 1 level. Nearby drainage areas unseeded during this time ranged from a deficit of 22 per cent to an increase of 19 per cent. Such a performance prompted Dallas water works officials to say they were convinced that seeding brought "a substantial increase" to the watershed area, and that their confidence was evident in the renewing of the contract with Krick.

Another scientific rainmaker was Dr. Wallace E. Howell, once a meteorologist at Harvard. He was hired by New York City to augment the rainfall of its reservoirs during the 1950–1951 water shortage. He seeded 36 times over a period of 31 weeks, and during that time the rainfall in the seeded area of watershed was 14 per cent higher than that of the surrounding, unseeded area. This meant an extra 15 billion gallons of water for the New York reservoir system, or enough to last about two weeks.

Howell put his cloud seeding to different use near Forestville, Quebec, in August, 1953. There he seeded an area for 10 days and brought rain that put out a fire in an area 50 by 100 miles. Another one of his programs was in Cuba for a sugar plantation owner, and 34 seeding operations with ground generators in 1952 produced a marked increase in rainfall on the target land area.

Down under in Australia, a land that never has enough rain in some areas, another series of cloud-seeding experiments was conducted by E. G. Bowen. It was his conclusion that cloud seeding by plane could possibly increase rainfall by from 5 per cent to 10 per cent, and that seeding could be done with both dry ice and water, depending on whether clouds were supercooled or warm. However, he found that ground-based generators did not work well in Australia. His considered opinion was that seeding would be economically feasible only in areas where extra rain could mean a great deal of extra money to farmers. For instance, one wheat-growing area produced an extra two million dollars for each additional inch of rain during August and September.

THE LOST DECADE

Dr. Irving Langmuir died in 1957 at the age of 76. He had lived to be part of artificial weather modification, and to predict for it a wonderful future of great benefit to mankind. But he died seeing the field in a state of shock and confusion, with reports from many organizations of reputable standing that there was no proved benefit in cloud seeding. Prime among the detractors of the work of Schaefer, Langmuir, Krick and other partisans, was the U.S. Weather Bureau itself.

It will be remembered that historically most meteorologists were opposed to man-made changes of the weather, and their skepticism was often heavily larded with caustic satire. This attitude prevailed among most of the nation's meteorologists through the 1940's and 1950's and well into the 1960's. A national weather-modification program was introduced in 1951 to a Weather Bureau that was not very "bullish," as a legislator said recently, on the subject of weather modification. A few small programs were funded, but even after the Eisenhower committee in 1957 reported that it was probable that rainmakers were increasing precipitation appreciably, government interest lagged far behind the enthusiasm of commercial rainmakers and the small band of scientists convinced that man could control the weather. Part of the reluctance stemmed from commendable scientific conservatism. The problem of possible dangers resulting from rash meddling with the weather was also something to be carefully considered, although a scientist convinced that rain-makers did no more to change the weather "than Indians beating on tom-toms" surely could not have been very fearful of meteoro-logical catastrophes induced by silver iodide. Whatever the cause, the past ten years has been called the "lost decade" by pioneers in weather modification.

Simply seeding a few clouds and having them grow into thunderstorms is not positive proof that the seeding did the job. The clouds may well have produced the storm unaided. Thus, much early and impressive work, including that of Dr. Langmuir and his weekly cycle of rain, was discounted. As to the weekly cycle, it was pointed out that man may have created this himself without help from silver iodide. Our cultural cycle is one of seven days, and the shutting down of factories, the driving of more miles on weekends by motorists, and other similar routine fluctuations may of themselves have altered the weather into a weekly cycle.

A key argument between the cloud seeder in the field and the meteorologist in his laboratory was the matter of statistical validity. Krick and others could demonstrate empirically that every year they seeded there was more than the average amount of rain, and that the seeded areas got more precipitation than upwind areas. But the meteorologist demanded sophisticated statistical proof depending on countless tests over many years of time.

RAINMAKING TODAY

The term "lost decade" is surely a relative one. Perhaps much more could indeed have been accomplished with more govern-ment help, but private weather makers themselves have not let too many clouds pass over or under their dry-ice bombs or smoke generators. Legislative hearings on new bills for weather modification pointed up this fact dramatically. Such experts have cloud seeders become that Dr. Wendell Mordy of the University of Nevada described for senators his tricky feat of punching out a Morse code "R" in the sky by selectively seeding clouds.

Describing the demonstration, which took place in the spring of 1966, Mordy said, "We dropped ice for a mile, stopped for a mile, went two miles, stopped for another mile, and then seeded for a third time." The "R," he said, could have stood for "Reno, research, or reclamation," and was plainly visible on the Meeks radar scope. Other rainmakers are spelling out dramatic successes with this cloud-seeding alphabet.

In 1959 there were thirty-six weather-modification projects reported by state, local, and commercial operators. This held fairly steady until 1965, when the total jumped to double the previous figure. In fiscal 1965, the latest year for which full reports are available, seventy-nine weather modification projects were reported in the Magnuson Report. Of these, seventy-one were privately financed, three by the Federal government, two by individual states, and three by universities. A few samples of the weather-changers' work follow:

Atmospherics Incorporated: To increase precipitation (California)
Brewer-Fisher Spray Service: Hail suppression (North Dakota)
Cloud Modification Service, Inc.: To increase precipitation and suppress hail (North Dakota)
Intermountain Weather, Inc.: To dissipate supercooled fog (Utah)
North American Weather Consultants of California: To increase snowpack (California)
Weather Engineering Corp.: To increase rain and snow for hydroelectric power generation; also projects to increase rain to protect forests (Canada)
Water Resources Development Corp.: To increase rain or snow (many states)
W. E. Howell Associates, Inc.: Rainfall stimulation for watersheds (Pennsylvania)

Irving P. Krick, Inc., of Texas: To increase rainfall for sugar-
    cane growing (Louisiana)
World Weather, Inc.: To increase water supply (Texas)
Bowman-Slope County Hail Suppression Association: To sup-
    press hail (North Dakota)
United Air Lines: To disperse supercooled fog (Idaho, Oregon)
Cold Regions Research & Engineering Laboratory: To increase
    airport visibility (Greenland, New Hampshire)

U.S. Department of the Interior

Field engineer for E. Bollay Associates ignites a silver-iodide generator
on the mountain slope at Snoqualmie Pass.

California had twelve projects, Colorado seven, Oregon six,
Louisiana, South Dakota, Utah, and Washington four each.
There were 27 states in all in which weather modification was
being carried out, and four of the projects were of a scope to
involve more than one state.

Dr. Krick's firm alone has now logged a total of more than two
million hours of silver-iodide generator operation in twenty-nine
of the United States, seven Canadian provinces, Mexico, Central
America, the West Indies, Spain, France, Italy, Sardinia, Israel,

Syria, North Africa, and the Congo. It has reported on close to two hundred projects. All this, according to Krick, is only a beginning. For example, he estimates that to increase the flow of the Colorado River by two million acre-feet a year by cloud seeding would cost in the neighborhood of one million dollars, or about fifty cents an acre-foot. One acre-foot is 325,851 gallons. The government's saline-water conversion planners are hoping some day to change salt water to fresh for about fifty cents for 1,000 gallons.

The two decades of modern rainmaking have been a frustrating paradox to proponents of weather control. Despite all the promise apparent in the artificial making of rain, the millennium has not yet come. Within two years of Schaefer's first small-scale demonstration, Dr. Langmuir had claimed to manipulate a hurricane, to bring down billions of gallons of rain, and even to cause a weekly cycle of precipitation in much of the United States. In the next eighteen years the rainmakers seemed to slip back down the precipice he had claimed to scale so boldly. Today, perhaps the plateau has been reached and the next twenty years will bear the fruit of rewards promised by seeding in 1947.

"Rain, rain, go away,
Come again some other day."

—Nursery Rhyme

6

The Weather Chasers

JUST as ancient man prayed and otherwise tried to bring rain, so he tried to rout storms that ruined his crops or infringed upon his war-making activities. The earliest would-be storm stoppers probably prayed, used magic, angrily shook fists, or shouted. Later, lances and arrows were hurled skyward to kill the storm. When gunpowder added to the arsenal of weaponry, cannon joined the effort at stopping wind, torrential rains, and damaging hail. Perhaps there were incantations and other attempts at dissipating fog for hunts or ceremonial purposes.

Cannon were advocated and tried for the opposite reason, that of bringing precipitation. The sound was believed a factor in weather as in the ringing of church bells to ward off hailstorms; some also thought that the smoke ring from the gun was effective. When rockets became available, these were added to the fray, and the practice persists today in many countries. As with rainmaking, storm chasing and fog dispersal on a scientific basis began in the 1940's, with the General Electric carbon-dioxide cloud-seeding experiments and by exploiting the other end of the temperature scale as pioneered during World War II by the British. Since it is simpler, we will discuss first the dispersal of fog.

Fog

There are three general types of fog: radiation, advection, and evaporation. Radiation fog occurs when the earth cools sufficiently to drop the temperature of the air above it below the condensation point. Advection fog is caused by warm moist air moving in over cold water or land. Evaporation fog results when sufficient moisture is added to an air mass to saturate it. This type of fog requires a warmer surface underlying cooler air, and is often frontal fog.

Fog can also be composed of either water or ice crystals. Ice fog, called "whiteout" in the Arctic, obviously occurs in cold climates. Water fog can also be cold fog. Such a "supercooled" fog exists at temperatures below freezing. Above this temperature a fog is called "warm." Suppression techniques vary depending on the temperature of the fog being treated.

Coastal regions and those adjacent to large inland bodies of water naturally breed more fog than dry regions. The mean number of days on which there is some fog along the west coast of the United States is sixty per year. San Francisco is famous for its fog, and that fog may have prevented Sir Francis Drake from discovering the great bay he sought in 1579. Point Reyes, California, averages 1,468 hours of fog yearly, but the foggiest spot is on the east coast. The Libby Islands off Maine average 1,554 hours a year, and in 1907 a discouraging 2,734 hours of fog were recorded at Seguin Light Station.

For ages traffic has been slowed or brought to a standstill by fog. A pedestrian can grope and fumble his way along, ships can slow speed or stop, and automobiles can do the same thing. But an airplane cannot park up in the air. When the cloud ceiling is less than 300 feet and visibility under ¾ mile, air traffic comes to a complete halt. Assuming that accidents are avoided despite the fog by canceling flights or by diverting to a clear landing field, there remains the high cost of such operations. Understandably there has been much effort for many decades to whip the fog problem.

U.S. Department of the Interior

University of Wisconsin personnel release a smoke bomb in Wyoming weather-modification studies on Elk Mountain.

In the 1920's electrified sand was tried on fog without much success. So much would have to be dropped that runways might resemble sand dunes! In 1935 a different approach was taken by meteorologist H. G. Houghton of M.I.T. Experimenting at Cape Cod, with warm advection fogs, Houghton and others tried two methods for ridding small areas of fog. In the first, highly concentrated calcium chloride solution was sprayed directly into fog blowing past the equipment. The second method used calcium chloride powder to dehumidify air in a large chamber. This dried air was then blown in and mixed with the fog.

According to the reports of the 1935 work, fog was cleared from an area more than 600 yards long, 30 to 50 yards wide, and to a height of at least 15 to 20 yards. Despite the success achieved, the idea was not developed any further than the preliminary tests, because of the expense, the unwieldiness of the equipment, and the corrosive qualities of the salt used to dry the air.

After all these exotic schemes, it is humbling to find that so lowly a method as a fire first tamed the fog menace.

FIDO

Fire has been used in many ways to alter the weather. We keep warm around a fire, and farmers burn smudgepots to warm their crops during freezing weather. But only in this century was fire used to dissipate low clouds or fog. As early as the 1920's, fog had been chased experimentally with heat, and in World War II the necessity for flying airplanes in all kinds of weather led to the first practical application of this principle.

A cloud forms when the air temperature falls below the dewpoint or saturation point of the air. Water vapor then condenses to form the tiny droplets of fog that plague the motorist and the flier. If the temperature is raised above the dewpoint, the droplets again become vapor and the air clears.

The British Isles have always been fogbound, and it was here that the first practical fog-dissipating scheme was put to work. The use of an acronym, or an abbreviation made up of first letters, was strained to the utmost with FIDO, standing for Fog, Investigations Dispersal Of. Simplicity itself, FIDO consisted of containers of fuel oil placed along the runways at airports. When fog swathed a field and it was necessary to bring a plane down,

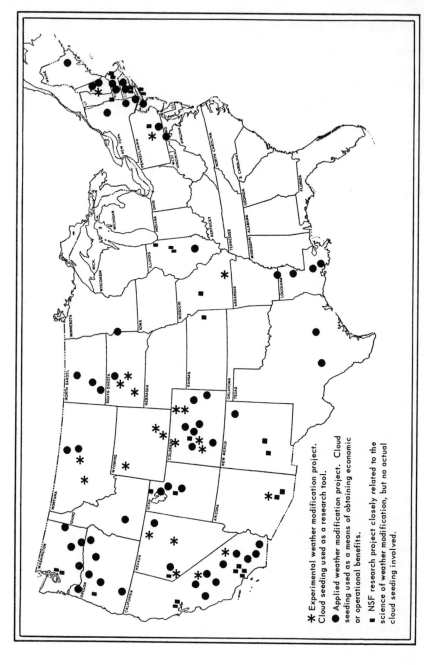

* Experimental weather modification project. Cloud seeding used as a research tool.

● Applied weather modification project. Cloud seeding used as a means of obtaining economic or operational benefits.

■ NSF research project closely related to the science of weather modification, but no actual cloud seeding involved.

National Academy of Sciences

mechanics hastily ignited the fuel and the intense heat literally burned the fog off for a few feet. Burning 6,000 gallons of oil for a single plane to land was an expensive proposition, however, and only wartime necessity made it a practical weather-modification system.

Following World War II, tests were conducted at the Landing Aids Experiment Station at Arcata, California, and also at Los Angeles International Airport. These tests did not prove practical. One reason was easily predictable; in view of the huge amounts of fuel required to burn off the fog it was not economically feasible to use except in a great emergency. A second reason was the "psychological effect on airline passengers," as a report described the problem. Slanting down for a landing amidst towering flames would be a harrowing finale to circling blindly in the fog. The burning oil also produced additional quantities of water in the atmosphere and sometimes added to the fog rather than alleviating it.

FIDO worked with both types of fog, cold and warm. Later, a less expensive method of dissipating cold, ice-crystal fog would be evolved using dry-ice seeding. For warm fog this method is useless, and the most recent attempts at handling it have gone back to the thermal method with more efficient burning techniques, as we shall see later in this chapter.

Cold Fog

When Vincent Schaefer's dry-ice seeding first proved it could dissipate a cloud, the cloud was a stratus layer. Fog is stratus cloud in contact with earth, so it was natural that the seeding technique be investigated for fog chasing. It was poetic too that an airplane brought the first encouraging proof that fog could be got rid of, since fog is one of the greatest hazards for aircraft.

While mere fog dissipation was generally forgotten in the grandiose rainmaking schemes of the late 1940's and early 1950's, some work was done by private organizations in the Pacific Northwest beginning in 1950. For obvious reasons, the government also sponsored research into the suppression of cold fog as an aid to military operations. Since fog is regional as well as seasonal it is not of pressing concern to any but the airlines faced with lost revenues. Many areas are not troubled with cold fogs. New York, for instance, has only about one hour a year of airport shutdown due to cold fog. But in Medford, Oregon, there are 207 hours a year. Spokane, Washington, has 159. Salt Lake City has 53 hours, Washington, D.C., 23 hours, and Denver 15 hours. These are average figures, and at times airports are closed for long periods by cold fogs. Cancellations of flights due to fog are estimated to cost airlines about $50 million a year.

In 1960 United Air Lines requested that the Federal Aviation Agency (F.A.A.) take the initiative in urging municipalities in the Northwest to undertake the dissipation of the cold fogs that frequently closed down their airports. The F.A.A. turned down this proposal, but in 1962 the airline itself began an active program. Intermountain Weather, a cloud-seeding firm, was hired to seed an area near Salt Lake City. Unfortunately—or fortunately, depending on where one sat—there was no dense cold fog at Salt Lake airport that year.

It happened that Vincent Schaefer was conducting cold-fog-seeding tests in Yellowstone Park in 1962. Here it was found that a bucket of water thrown into the air produced an immediate cloud. On his way home, Schaefer passed through Salt Lake City where he photographed the schedule board of the airlines, show-ing "All Flights Cancelled Account Weather."

The following year United again contracted with Intermoun-tain for seeding at Salt Lake City, and with Mercy Flights, Inc., at Medford, Oregon. During the winter, sixteen fog-seeding flights were made, eight at each airport. Crushed dry ice was dropped into the fog deck in a pattern corresponding to the runway. This meant some blind flying for the pilot, and the possibility that he might have to fly to an alternate field if the seeding did not work.

In 1963 and 1964 another seven airports were added to those served by fog dispersal service. During the winter of 1964 and 1965 a total of seventy-four seeding flights were conducted, and permitted 269 takeoffs or landings of commercial craft that could

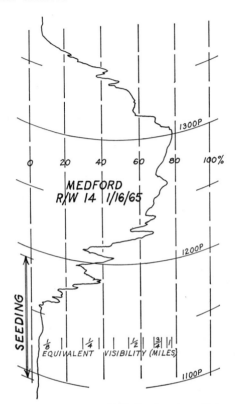

Transmissometer trace during and following seeding at Medford, Oregon, on January 16, 1965. Transmissivity reading (in per cent) at beginning of seeding is equivalent to visibility of 1/8 mile. Landing minimums (1/2 mile) occurred when transmissivity reached 55 per cent.

not have been accomplished otherwise. Nearly 5,700 passengers were handled. The costs to the seven participating airports were $17,000, about $150 per flight hour of fog seeding.

In the three years that seeding of cold fog has been done at the Northwest cities, United Air Lines alone handled an extra 8,380 passengers. The cost per extra passenger of the seeding is about $3, indicating the great financial return of the operation. United

Air Lines estimates that its return is about $5 for every dollar spent on seeding. The coming of the jets and their expensive operation hastened work in fog dispersal.

Cold-fog dry-ice seeding is about 80 per cent successful. Seeding flights can be arranged on three hours' notice, and planes may be on a standby basis. The clearing of the fog is timed to coincide with the planned departure or arrival of a flight or bank of flights. The seeding flight lasts about one hour, and drops between 100 and 400 pounds of dry ice into the fog overlying the airport.

While cold-fog dispersal thus far has been done mainly for aircraft takeoffs and landings, there are other applications. For example, United Air Lines has had requests from shipowners concerning the elimination of fog at critical bridgeheads along busy ship canals. Highways could benefit similarly, and farming operations could be speeded by clearing fogs. A small city in the Northwest "manufactured a fair day" for itself, by applying the fog-dispersal technique on a larger scale. This might be done for sale days, sports events, or other special affairs. It is possible too that smog conditions may be alleviated by similar methods, although no progress has been reported as yet in this direction.

Work continues by United Air Lines and others on means for dispersing warm fogs. If and when successful, this will mean tremendous savings for the airlines at Los Angeles, San Francisco, New York, Washington, and other airports plagued with warm fogs. It will also mean better service for passengers.

United is experimenting in Texas with a chemical approach to warm-fog dissipation. The University of Pittsburgh uses a "heat-blitz" method in which a hot-air generator below ground feeds air through louvers and ducts to the edge of the runway.

Fog Dispersal in France

Some outstanding work in fog dispersal has also been done in France by the Paris Airport Authority. This work differs from that in the United States in that neither dry ice nor silver iodide is used as a dissipation agent. In 1954, M. R. Serpolay showed that by spraying liquids with low boiling points, such as propane, the same results could be obtained as with dry ice seeding. The winter of 1953–1954 had been an especially bad one for fog at French airports, and there was much interest in fog-dissipation systems.

An engineer named J. Olivier demonstrated in January, 1956, the Serpolay technique at the Lyon-Brion airport, spraying the propane from ground-based nozzles. Olivier also developed a method of dispersing warm fogs by spraying hygroscopic and electrified particles instead of propane. During the winter of 1956–1957, tests were conducted using the electrified particle method at Orly Airport. These tests were not carried out successfully, and Olivier died in 1957. Serpolay, a scientist on the French Research Council, then joined with the researchers at the Paris Airport Authority and has carried out fog-dispersal trials and routine operation since 1958.

Ten mobile stations sprayed propane into the foggy air around Orly during the winter of 1958–1959, resulting in visibility improvement of from two to three times. Ninety-one hours of fog were sprayed and some success achieved. The following year forty fixed spray units took the place of the mobile units and results confirmed the hopes of the preceding year. However, there was only five hours of fog during the winter for the experimenters to work on.

On January 18, 1961, the propane seeding system cut the fog enough to permit eighteen takeoffs and two landings that otherwise could not have been made safely. By January of 1964 the system permitted ninety-six takeoffs and seventy-six landings during a three-day period of sixty hours of dense fog. The propane seeding increased visibility in the airport area from 150 yards to 1,200 yards. So successful and reliable was the system that it was classed semioperational in November, 1964. On Christmas Eve of that year it permitted ninety-five takeoffs and seventy-four landings from runways that would have otherwise been closed.

An operational system was designed, to be completed in 1967. It is considered a paying proposition, like the dry-ice seeding in the United States, and will permit an average of from 200 to 250 extra aircraft operations each year. Sixty spraying units will surround the airport, with nozzles capable of varying the rate of sprayed propane from about 5 to 40 pounds per hour. Each tank will hold 1,300 pounds of propane, sufficient for more than 30 hours of continuous operation at maximum output.

As pointed out by the Paris Airport Authority, the propane ground-based system has advantages over the aerial seeding method. There is no standby expense of aircraft or attendant danger to such a craft.

Propane seeding works only on cold fog. For warm fog, the French experimented first with Olivier's hygroscopic and electrified-particle method. The hygroscopic particles were water droplets saturated with sodium chloride, or salt. Early tests seemed promising but were not practical, so effort was switched to the use of heat to evaporate rather than coalesce the fog particles. This work began in 1958.

The first warm fog dispersal units were much like the British FIDO oil burners, and suffered the same problems of high operating cost. Next, the French tried hot-air blowers, which did not work well; and turbo-jet engines—which did. The United States Air Force had experimented in 1951 with turbo-jet fog dispersal at Arcata Air Base in California with some success. Now the French put it to good use, exploiting the so-called "Coanda" effect of the jet's air blast in hugging the ground when the jet was tilted slightly downward. A tilt of 4 degrees was found to be the best compromise for adherence and range of the air blast.

In still air the thermal-fog dissipation method works well, the French have found. However, operation in all wind conditions has not been achieved and warm-fog dissipation is not a practical operation as yet.

Other Fog Research

The Cold Regions Research and Engineering Laboratories has used rockets and balloons to carry seeding agents into fog or Arctic "whiteout" areas. Nucleating agents such as phloroglucinol, urea, dry ice, and liquid propane spray were tried. Also the

United Air Lines

Small fog-seeding plane poses before airliner which landed thanks to dry-ice fog dispersal.

downwash from a helicopter was tried on warm fog. Propane seeding of cold fog was done in the Hanover-Lebanon area in New Hampshire, and at Camp Century and Thule Air Base in Greenland.

At the Air Force Cambridge Research Laboratories, fog experiments have included the "cloudbuster" system, in which an airborne apparatus converts liquid carbon dioxide automatically into pellets and disperses them into stratus clouds.

Kites, vertical fans, and drone aircraft are also being used in fog-dispersal studies. One project, conducted at Cape Cod where Houghton did his work some thirty years ago, is called CAT-FEET, apparently from the descriptive used in the Carl Sandburg poem, "Fog." An infrared heating system has reportedly been tested at Travis Air Force Base in northern California.

Bernard Vonnegut conducted tests in 1956 in which oil was

used in a completely different way for fog suppression. A mist of oil that had been highly charged electrically was blown by an airplane propeller into the natural fog. This charged oil formed the upper plate of an electrical condenser, the earth itself being the lower. It was hoped that water droplets suspended between the two plates would become charged and coalesce into large enough drops to fall to the ground. Unfortunately the phenomena of "corona" and "arcing" occurred. This electrical short circuit through the air neutralized the charge before a high

Aéroport de Paris

Propane fog-dispersal unit installed at Orly Field.

enough electrical potential could be reached to precipitate the water droplets.

In 1961, G. E. Hagen tried another approach to the electrical dissipation of fog. This was simply a highly charged wire installed upwind so that the fog would drift across it, also causing coalescence of small drops into large because of the electrical field. Again the charge leaked to the ground without accomplishing fog dispersal.

Theoretical research was carried out in 1962 to find if it would be beneficial to seed fog with carbon black. This material would then soak up more solar heat and warm the fog enough to evaporate the droplets of fog. It was calculated that seeding clouds at the rate of 40 kilograms (88 pounds) of carbon black per square kilometer (⅓ square mile) would clear the air in ten minutes. Practical success was not attained.

In Chile's Altacama Desert in the northern regions, the water from fogs is extracted by 4-foot frames strung with nylon thread. In a year some 220 gallons per square yard of framework is produced. This same method has been used in New Jersey in an attempt to rid highways of fog.

Russia is reported to be doing experimental work in precipi-

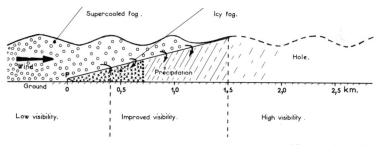

Aéroport de Paris

Diagram of effects of propane seeding of supercooled fog. Propane introduced at Point P.

tating warm fogs with sound waves. Sound waves of from 1.5 to 5 kilocycles per second and intensities of 0.5 watts per square centimeter appear to precipitate the droplets within seconds.

In Japan meteorologists have seeded warm stratus clouds with water in an attempt to effect collisions of drops and the eventual "rainout" of moisture. An even simpler method is that of using a forest to screen out much of the water in advection fogs.

In United States fog studies laboratory tests were made on treatment of hygroscopic particles so they would not collect droplets, and of the droplets themselves with material to prevent coalescence. Such treated drops bounce off *water* instead of mingling with it. No practical success in fog dispersal has been

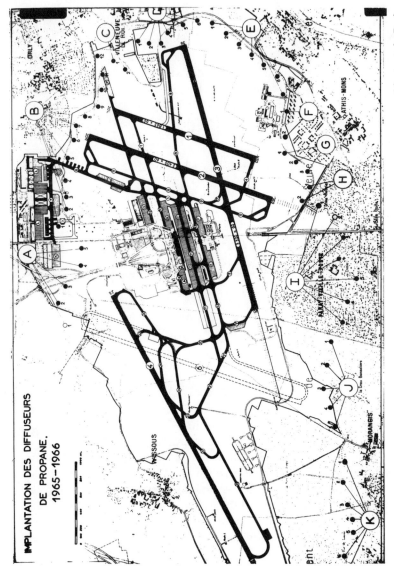

IMPLANTATION DES DIFFUSEURS DE PROPANE. 1965-1966

Aéroport de Paris

reported with this method, but Japanese researchers have coated fog droplets with mono-molecular films to *preserve* artificial fog for farmers and horticulturists.

HURRICANE SEEDING

The name "hurricane" probably comes from the West Indian or Central American word *huracan,* for great wind, or *Hunrakan,* the god of stormy weather. Tropical cyclones originate in all tropical oceans except the South Atlantic. In the North Atlantic they occur around the Cape Verde Islands, the western Caribbean and the Gulf of Mexico from May through November.

There is still mystery surrounding the birth of a hurricane. Moist, unstable air and curving winds are the culprits, but these are so abundant that experts wonder seriously why many *more* hurricanes don't start. There are a number of theories, including the convectional, the equatorial front, the easterly wave, and others. All involve Coriolis force, and this means that the hurricanes cannot begin nearer than about 6 degrees to the Equator, where the force is much less. The farther from the Equator, the more Coriolis force and the more hurricanes.

The eye of the hurricane ranges from 7 to 20 miles in diameter. It may be swathed in cirrus cloud, or may be clear, with the sun shining brightly or stars winking down. At the eye the pressure is the lowest (the official record being 26.35), the temperature the highest, and the humidity the lowest. The air is thought to be descending in the eye of the storm. A hurricane may be 500 miles across, and it moves at an average of only about 12 miles an hour. Since the hurricane feeds on water, it dies out over land but usually not before doing great damage.

In 1737 a hurricane, or typhoon, rather, killed an estimated quarter of a million people in Asia and destroyed 20,000 ships and boats. From 1864 to 1882, three typhoons in India killed 385,000 people, and as recently as 1942, 40,000 were killed in a single tropical storm. The worst hurricane disaster in the United States occurred at Galveston, Texas, on September 8, 1900. Six thousand people were drowned.

In 1928 more than 1,800 were killed in a hurricane that struck Florida, and in 1938 a New England hurricane took a toll of 600 dead. A Texas-Louisiana hurricane killed nearly 400 in 1957. The average hurricane has a life of ten days, and in that time is estimated to use enough energy to electrify the United States for one million years. A mature hurricane consumes as much energy in a second as twenty small atom bombs, thus the suggestion to use such energy in an attempt to kill the storm makes about as much sense as primitive men trying to do the job with arrows and gunfire. Even H-bombs are not thought capable of the job and of course their use would add to the complications by polluting the atmosphere and possibly making long-range changes in the weather.

Hurricanes seem to have earned feminine names for their unpredictable ways. In the George Stewart book, *Storm,* a meteorologist has the habit of calling hurricanes by girl's names, and the idea was picked up during World War II by real meteorologists in the Army and Navy. The first hurricane of the season is called Alma, for example, the second Beulah, and so on through the alphabet. In the Pacific, a long series of names is used, since many more storms occur there.

Early in the rainmaking game it was learned that a cloud seeder could defeat his purpose by using too much dry ice on his cloud target. As Langmuir explained, this resulted in so many ice crystals that there wasn't enough moisture in the cloud to feed them all. Thus they stayed small and did not lead to precipitation. Here was a kind of cold-storage system for rain that someday might keep water in the sky rather than in a reservoir on earth.

When Project Cirrus aviators began to carve their huge canyons in cloud decks, Langmuir predicted that it might be possible to rid the country of the hurricanes that yearly kill many and damage millions in property. Overseeding the storm clouds of a tropical hurricane should release great quantities of heat and cause it to lose energy quickly. Its strength gone, the storm would then dissipate without doing any harm.

From October 10 to 15, the second worst hurricane of 1947 roared across Florida from west to east and headed out to sea. It seemed to be dissipating when three planes from Project Cirrus caught up with it, one of them a B-29 and the others B-17's. Three runs were made and 180 pounds of dry ice—costing about $7—dropped some distance from the eye. "Pronounced modification of the cloud deck seeded" was reported but nothing special seemed to happen. The planes swung west for home. The storm was then about 400 miles off the Georgia coast and moving slowly north. After the seeding, however, the rain increased and the hurricane veered westward. Soon after, it struck the city of Savannah and wreaked havoc to the tune of about $5 million in property damage.

Here was a result that to many seemed as conclusive as Langmuir's later rainmaking at Socorro, New Mexico. The scientist himself believed that seeding had changed the course of the hurricane, embarrassing as that announcement was in light of the damage done by such weather meddling. Others disagreed, and cited the similar meanderings of a hurricane in 1906 as proof that the change in course was nature's and not attributable to Project Cirrus' cloud seeding.

Until 1821 even meteorologists didn't know what a hurricane was, except that it was a terrible storm with very high winds and rain. In that year a New England shopkeeper named William C. Redfield was surprised to notice that a September hurricane had blown trees down in one direction in part of Connecticut and the opposite direction elsewhere. He reasoned correctly that the great storm must have been a whirlwind. Ten years later, after compiling a mass of data from newspapers and ships' logs, Redfield published a paper that accurately described a hurricane as a cyclonic storm; that is, one in which the winds spiral (counterclockwise direction north of the Equator and clockwise south of it) about a calm center or "eye." He also believed that despite the gale winds that accompanied hurricanes, the storms themselves moved quite slowly.

For more than a hundred years not much more was learned about the structure of hurricanes, however, and when Project Cirrus seeded the one off Georgia it was truly a shot in the dark. Not until 1943, for example, had an airplane flown into a hurricane. Then Colonel Joseph P. Duckworth of the Army Air

Corps flew a single-engine training plane into the eye of a hurricane. With radar came a powerful new instrument for studying hurricanes, and weathermen soon learned the telltale swirling signature of the storm on radar scopes, with the distinct eye at the center of the cyclonic system.

In 1950 Langmuir said that he thought the time was ripe for beginning an intensive study of tropical hurricanes. He thought that silver-iodide generators used at sea level might make it possible to modify the storms, and even prevent them from reaching land.

In 1955 two particularly destructive hurricanes called Connie and Diane caused a billion dollars in damage to the east coast, and soon after that the National Hurricane Center was established in Miami. Hurricane-hunter planes patrolled the ocean on the lookout for incipient storms, of which about ten develop a year. Once found, a new hurricane is carefully tracked and warnings can be given enough ahead of time for the cities to board up and otherwise get ready for the blow. Occasionally a hurricane plane is damaged by the gales within the storm, and one was lost completely with all the crew.

As radar plainly shows, a hurricane consists of a generally clear eye, surrounded by a great band of clouds that spiral about it. These rainbands were unknown until radar, which detects the presence of water in clouds, showed them. Now they are thought to be the mechanism that feeds energy to the central circular wall of cloud that is the heart of the storm. The churning, violent thunderclouds at the center of the hurricane may reach up to 50,000 feet.

With aircraft, radar, and balloon instruments, scientists of the National Hurricane Research Laboratory (NHRL) have found that large quantities of supercooled water vapor may be present in hurricane clouds. A relatively small "chimney" of cloud, located on the right side of the eye as one faces the direction of storm movement, seems to serve as the primary energy cell of the storm, conducting the inflow of moist warm air up through a narrow "hot tower" and out at the top as a "cirrus primary." On the left side of the eye is a less energetic, and lower, vertical cloud build-up that leads upward to a "cirrus secondary" with

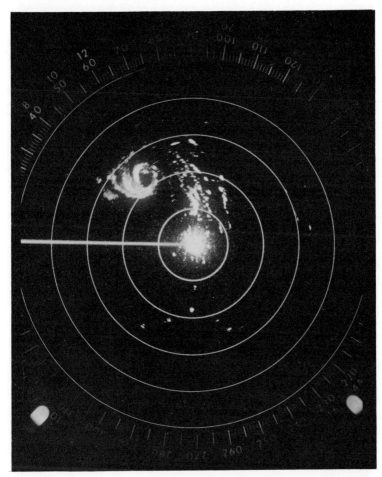

U.S. Department of Commerce, Weather Bureau

This is Hurricane Cleo taken by the Weather Bureau's high-powered radar, August 27, 1964, 02:54 A.M., EST, at Key West, Florida, when the eye of the storm was over Miami, Florida.

top at about 40,000 feet. Outward from the eye are lesser build-ups of cumulonimbus clouds from 10,000 to 30,000 feet high.

As more was learned about the complex structure of the

hurricane it became apparent that simply flying into the storm and dumping dry ice was a most unscientific and wasteful procedure to follow. Not until 1961, after initial experiments with Hurricane Esther, did the Department of Commerce join forces with the U.S. Navy in Project Stormfury, a descendant of Project Cirrus that Langmuir had launched almost fifteen years earlier.

Also in 1961 Dr. Pierre Saint Amand of the Naval Ordnance Test Station at China Lake, California, developed an improved silver-iodide generator called the Alecto. This generator is dropped from the plane and falls through the cloud to be seeded, ejecting iodide smoke as it drops and quickly spreading the sublimation nuclei. The device seemed excellent for use in hurricane-seeding experiments, and it was used in the Hurricane Esther tests.

On September 16 and 17, 1961, U.S. Navy aircraft patrolled a pie-shaped sector of the storm to the right of its eye for three hours, measuring various parameters. A Navy A3B plane then approached the center of the hurricane and dropped eight of the Alecto generators from 43,000 feet. The smoke rapidly traveled downward through 4 miles of cloud, from their tops to the freezing level.

Observation planes monitored the clouds following the seeding, using radar of two types. One showed ice crystals, small raindrops, and snow; the other only water droplets. Within twenty minutes after the plane had seeded the clouds, the radar screen showing water drops only went blank, indicating that they had changed to ice or become much smaller drops of water. It was two hours before the rainwall built itself back.

NHRL was eager to continue such experiments the following year, but nature refused to cooperate. The only thing accomplished was a "dry run" for practice in Hurricane Daisy off the Florida coast. Strict rules had been set up as to where a hurricane must be for it to be safe to seed it. Finally, on August 23, 1963, the hurricane planes seeded Hurricane Beulah northeast of the island of San Juan. Apparently the iodide failed to go where it was supposed to, or else it had no effect. However, on the next day another attempt was made and this time, for the first time—or second, if Langmuir is to be given the credit he assumed—man seemed to nudge a gigantic storm. Soon after the seeding operation was carried out, the pressure of the air in the eye rose, and the area of maximum winds moved away from the storm center. Scientists pointed out that this shift *might* have been natural, caused by meteorological oscillations they knew nothing of.

An experiment in the seeding of isolated cumulus cloud was carried out by NHRL planes from August 17 to 21, and the seeded clouds were observed to grow at a rapid rate, while control clouds remained as before.

Again in 1965 the cumulus-seeding experiments were carried out, this time on more clouds than in 1963. Seeded clouds grew an average of 5,000 feet higher than did the unseeded ones, and the probability that this was a chance occurrence was calculated at less than 1 in 1,000.

It was impossible to conduct the full-scale hurricane tests in 1965 because no storms moved into the proper area. To some it seemed that the way to prevent hurricane damage was to permit seeding only over land; that way the perverse storms would never do any harm.

For 1966 it was planned to seed storms in the eyewall, and also the rainbands. Further restrictions were placed on the operation in that no hurricane could be seeded if it might reach a populated area within thirty-six hours. Plans were made to seed the eyewall five times at two-hour intervals, with a large number of Alecto units dropped on each run. Monitoring would begin three hours prior to the first seeding, and continue for six hours after the last, a total of seventeen hours in all.

The rainband seeding was to be done to attempt to find some link between normal convective activity found in a cumulus storm, and the further developed hurricane activity. Seeding the eyewall was expected to release heat as the water droplets froze. This might release a chain reaction that could change the course of the structure of the storm. But again in 1966 NHRL was doomed to disappointment. Hurricanes were born, rampaged, and died. Although the entire team stood by for Hurricane Faith in late August, the storm moved into the forbidden zone and seeding could not be attempted.

The cloud seeding of a hurricane is a big operation, and requires a sizable fleet of planes. DC-6's and C-54's record meteorological observations from 1,500 feet to 35,000 feet. A Super-Constellation controls all activity, and also makes measurements including those from rockets it launches for gathering data as much as 25,000 feet over the aircraft. And A3B Skywarriors make the actual Alecto generator drops. Air Force C-130 Hercules are used for dropsonde measurements, and special high-altitude planes perform wind observations and photograph the experiments.

Tornado Suppression

"Tornado" is a Spanish word, perhaps deriving from *tronada,* meaning "thunderstorm." A tornado is a rotating storm, similar to a hurricane, but much smaller, shorter-lived, and more violent. Rising currents caused by the sun's heat are thought to trigger tornadoes when other conditions such as winds and cloud cover are right. The diameter of the funnel ranges from a few feet to a mile, and winds about it may reach 300 miles an hour with updrafts of 200 miles an hour inside the funnel.

The tornado, also called a cyclone or twister, moves at about 20 to 40 miles an hour erratically along the ground, with the funnel sometimes lifting from contact with the earth. Average path length is about 300 miles and direction is to the northeast. The worst single tornado on record is that which struck St. Louis, Missouri, on May 27, 1896. Damage of about $10 million was done, and more than 300 people were killed.

In 1884 tornadoes killed 800 in the southern and central states. In 1925 almost 800 were killed, and in 1936, 500 were killed. Tornadoes in 1953 killed 234 people and did almost $100 million damage.

Many years ago a hopeful inventor suggested a device for blasting a tornado out of existence. This weather bomb would be

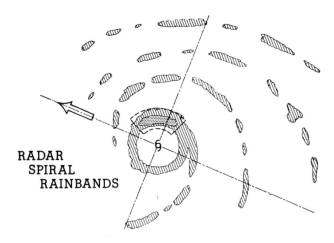

**RADAR
SPIRAL
RAINBANDS**

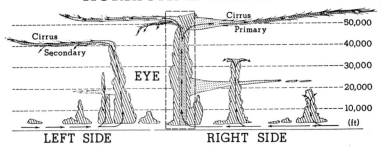

HURRICANE MODEL

Primary Energy Cell ("Hot Towers")　Convective Clouds　Altostratus　Cirrus

Environmental Science Services Administration

The hurricane model. The primary energy cell (convective chimney) is located in the area enclosed by the broken line.

hung on a high pole southwest of town (the direction from which tornadoes are supposed to come) and would be triggered by some atmospheric sensing device. Recent estimates of the power involved in a typical tornado indicate that an H-bomb would be needed hanging on that pole.

According to Bernard Vonnegut, a typical tornado funnel is kept going by a power equal to one-third the total electrical generating capacity of the United States. About twenty tons of

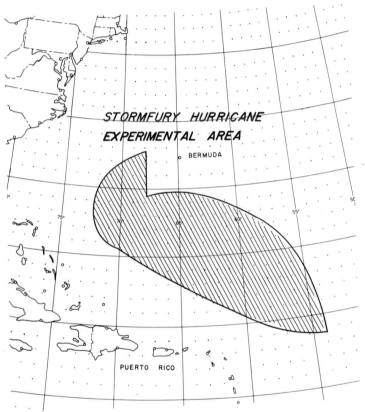

Environmental Science Services Administration

Project Stormfury experiments permitted only within the shaded area as a protection to populated areas.

high explosives a second would have to be detonated to match the tornado's awesome fury.

A different and less noisy approach to tornado taming is

suggested by some evidence that a strong air temperature inversion at about two kilometers altitude is likely to produce tornadoes. Why not burn fuel on the ground and heat the lower layers and thus eliminate the dangerous inversion? One reason is that to do this over one midwestern township suspected of harboring an incipient tornado would require all the nation's electric power channeled into heaters for three hours. However, men who dare to tackle a mighty hurricane with its huge store of energy surely won't be daunted by the tornado which is a tiny version of the much larger tropical storm. Just as silver iodide acts as a trigger to upset the delicately balanced forces of nature, so the storm-tamer seeks a mechanism for performing the work of a catalyst on the tornado. One possibility lies in lightning, and Bernard Vonnegut thinks that some slight alteration of the electrical balance in the storms that spawn tornadoes might delay or suppress their unruly children.

HAIL SUPPRESSION

Hail is formed by the freezing of water drops in a thundercloud. Vertical currents carry the ice ball high into the sky until it is heavy enough to fall. Descending, it partially melts, and if sliced in two shows successive build-ups of ice, like the layers of an onion. Ordinarily hail is of a size to be felt but not to inflict much damage on the human person, but there are hailstones as large as golf balls and, in some cases, grapefruit. In 1928 a hailstone 17 inches around and weighing 1½ pounds fell at Potter, Nebraska. Occasionally a luckless person is struck by such a lethal weapon and killed, but damage generally is restricted to crops.

Hail insurance is costly enough to be prohibitive in many areas, and can run as high as 25 per cent of the value of the crop. An indication of the cost of hail damage is the record of $15 million loss sustained in 1951 in the state of Kansas alone.

Hail comes all too often to suit the pocketbooks of farmers in many places about the world. Wheat ranches in Canada and the northern United States and grape vineyards in Italy are among

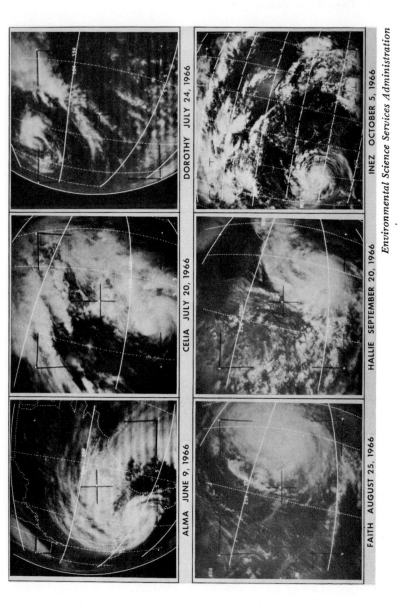

ALMA JUNE 9, 1966   CELIA JULY 20, 1966   DOROTHY JULY 24, 1966

FAITH AUGUST 25, 1966   HALLIE SEPTEMBER 20, 1966   INEZ OCTOBER 5, 1966

Environmental Science Services Administration

Some of the Atlantic hurricanes of 1966, photographed from space by ESSA satellites.

those affected. We have noted that the ringing of church bells was long thought to be of value in dissipating hail. The use of cannon for "hail shooting" was first tried in the seventeenth century in the French wine district of Beaujolais, but became general in the late nineteenth century.

By the turn of this century Italians had adoped a more "scientific" method. Antihail guns, giant artillery pieces with barrels like old-fashioned phonographs, blasted a doughnut-shaped

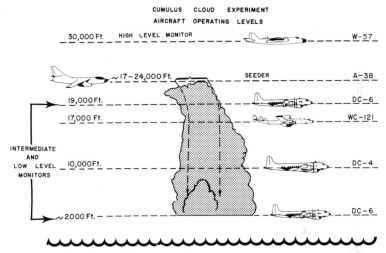

Environmental Science Services Administration

Aircraft types and altitudes flown in hurricane-seeding experiments.

charge of hot air skyward when a blank was fired. An old illustration shows a dozen of the weather weapons in the town square at Padua, and some 2,500 were in use before it was proved that they were of no value except to build the confidence of the farmer and line the pockets of their manufacturers.

Various theories have been offered to explain the working of the hail gun. One of these says that the shock wave of the gun breaks up the updrafts causing hail. Another suggests that the shock wave freezes supercooled water drops, although how this prevents hail does not seem clear. One report in 1938 claimed that supercooled water drops existed between 5,000 and 10,000 feet altitude in southern Europe, where hail guns were used. Proponents of hail cannon insisted its shock wave reached to 6,000 feet altitude, thus into the area of the supercooled drops.

Superseding the hail cannon a number of years ago were rockets used in Italy. At first these were hardly more than Fourth-of-July pyrotechnics, but as early as 1937 improved rockets were being fired from aircraft and success claimed for them in hail reduction. Rockets have also been used in France, Switzerland, and South Africa.

The theory advanced for the effectiveness (which has not been conclusively demonstrated) of hail rockets involves shock-wave action on the internal structure of the hailstone. Such rockets are said to be effective over an area of about 500 yards in diameter, and to produce "mushy" hailstones which do not do the damage of natural ones. In Italy alone more than one million hail rockets have reportedly been fired.

More modern and scientifically sound rockets now used incorporate about two pounds of explosive, with about 2 per cent of silver iodide added as a seeding agent. Cheaply made of cardboard, these rockets reach altitudes as high as 5,000 feet.

Russian weathermen claim to be able to identify those clouds actively producing hailstones; they use radar techniques to accomplish this. Once having located the danger spot, the Russians lob artillery shells at it, and these explode and spread silver iodide through the cloud. This seeding is thought to cause so many tiny ice crystals that none grow large enough to produce hailstones. However, some researchers believe that hail forms from liquid water drops, and they fear that seeding could produce even more hailstones.

The Russian shells place from 400 to 1,000 grams of silver iodide in each thunderstorm, and results are claimed to prove the effectiveness of the barrage. However, some scientists feel there is insufficient data to prove statistically that there is benefit from the seeding.

Experiments and commercial operations aimed at suppressing

U.S. Department of Commerce, Weather Bureau

Tornadoes like this one can be wholesale killers. The twisters can strike in all fifty of the United States.

hail in the United States, France, Switzerland, Bavaria, and Argentina do not use the pinpoint aiming technique of the Russians, but seed the cloud generally. Ground-based iodide generators or rockets carry the material into the storm area. Scientists still give little or no credit to rockets unless they contain a seeding agent.

The difficulty of analyzing results is shown in a five-year series of tests in Argentina. Lumping all the data seems to show a hail reduction over the entire period; breaking the tests down into frontal and nonfrontal thunderstorms indicates a decrease in hail damage of 70 per cent for frontal seeding but a 100 per cent *increase* in nonfrontal storms. Thus it would seem that seeding

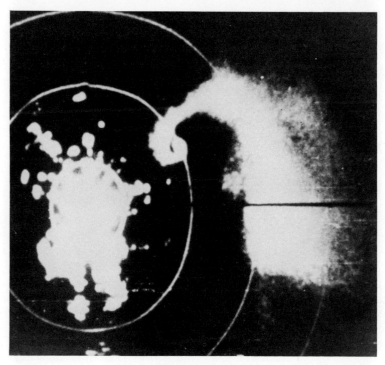

U.S. Department of Commerce, Weather Bureau

Sometimes tornadoes have a radar "fingerprint" as shown here. Weathermen can determine a tornado's speed and direction of movement by tracking it on a radar scope.

should not be used for nonfrontal storms.

In Switzerland the late Dr. R. Saenger conducted a seven-year series of hail-suppression tests, using ground-based generators. Analysis showed that there were 68 per cent more hail-days in the storms seeded than those not seeded.

Hail suppression in France has been carried on since 1951 and covers an area of some 27,000 square kilometers. Here, instead of trying to compute the statistics, the directors of the program rely on an "effectiveness factor," or ratio of paid hail insurance to total insured capital. Hail damage in the covered area has been

U.S. Department of Commerce, Weather Bureau

Hailstones this size can be lethal weapons.

less than average since 1959, except for 1963, and the French feel that the program is worthwhile.

Much of the work on hail suppression has been done in Alberta, Canada, one of the worst hail regions in the world, with hail swaths up to 15 miles wide and 100 miles long. As a result, hail insurance premiums are from 12 per cent to 22 per cent of the crop value. With hail suppression, losses in recent years have been cut to half the average of the forty-six years of records preceding the introduction of cloud seeding.

In the summer of 1966 some two dozen agencies in the United States cooperated in "Project Hailswath," conducted near Rapid City, South Dakota. This $172,000 pilot program featured scientists sporting "Help Stamp Out Hail" badges. During the test period less hail and more rain fell, although the scientists admitted that firm conclusions could not be drawn from such a small sampling.

Weather modification is commonly thought of as rainmaking, but the other side of the coin is also of great importance. The dispersal of fog, the suppression of hail, and the taming of storms are examples of weather chasing that can do as much good as weather making. Like the witch doctor of old, the modern weather modifier seeks talismans to "eat the clouds" as well as to squeeze the moisture from them.

7

Lightning Suppression

A DRAMATIC and frightening phenomenon associated with storms is lightning. The ancients attributed these vivid and noisy thunderbolts to Jove, who hurled them earthward at his pleasure to chastise his human subjects. Early Norsemen believed that lightning was sparks from mighty Thor's hammer, and pointed to the iron fragments found in the earth after a siege of shooting stars.

Benjamin Franklin began the job of pinning down the lightning in 1752 when he proved with his famous and risky experiment with kite-string and key that thunderbolts were made up of the same electrons as laboratory electricity, then so popular with scientist and showman.

Today we know that there are scientific rather than mythical reasons for the lightning that accompanies thunderstorms, but as recently as 1930 the idea of lightning as a creation of living beings persisted. At that time three charges of malicious lightning making were filed against witch doctors of the Kgatla tribe in what was then Bechuanaland Protectorate. One case was allegedly murder by lightning, and the accused admitted that he had indeed directed a lightning flash against his victim.

Our knowledge that no supernatural hand propels bolts of lightning from above has not lessened in any way their fantastic power—power that can kill and destroy. In 1782 the priest to the Duke of Kent was reportedly cured of paralysis by being struck by lightning, but this was a rare exception. Each year about 500 Americans lose their lives as victims of lightning. Of these, some 400 are men and boys and only 100 women and girls. This is because the male is more likely to be out in the open, engaged in sports or work when storms strike. An additional 1,300 are injured.

Animals die in even greater numbers, and in a single Utah storm 500 sheep were killed by lightning. Each year there are some 10,000 lightning-caused forest fires in the western part of America which destroy 16 million acres of timber.

Lightning, then, is not just a noisy and colorful display in the heavens, but a potent environmental force to be carefully studied so that man may reckon with it. The serious investigations now being made toward modifying lightning—as a part of weather— really began centuries ago.

History of Lightning

Fear of lightning is probably as old as man. Mistletoe, so important in mythology, was considered not natural but an aftermath of lightning. Later, a shrub called "Christ's letter" was carried as a charm against fatal harm from lightning. And thorn bushes were used in homes to guard against lightning. But there were wise men who doubted the effectiveness of such talismans and in 42 B.C. Publilius Syrus said, "It is vain to look for a defense against lightning."

Early in the 4th century A.D. Barbara Dioscorus, a Christian convert, was beheaded by her father. Lightning struck and killed him, and the martyred Barbara became patron saint for protection against thunder, lightning, and fire. As late as 1940 a portrait of Santa Barbara hung in the office of the Chief of the U.S. Navy Bureau of Ordnance in Washington, D.C.

Since lightning was considered a weapon flung earthward by wrathful gods, early man considered humans so killed as having incurred the anger of the heavens. Such victims were usually buried with little or no ceremony, and sometimes their graves were walled around as a shrine to the lightning hurler. Animals killed by lightning were considered unclean, and were not eaten.

So convinced were the peasants that bell ringing warded off lightning that many unfortunate bell ringers were killed by lightning. Charlemagne is said to have issued an edict prohibiting bell ringing during thunderstorms. As late as 1786 the Parliament in Paris had to reissue the ruling. Because of their height and isolation, church steeples made excellent "lightning rods" and from 1750 to 1783 in Europe there were recorded cases of 386 towers being struck and 103 ringers killed.

It was once the custom to store munitions in the vaults beneath churches, and in 1796 lightning struck the Church of St. Nazaire in Brescia and triggered the detonation of 100 tons of gunpowder. Some 3,000 people were killed. In 1856 4,000 or more people died when a similar cache was struck by lightning at the Church of St. Jean on the Island of Rhodes. This, remember, was long after the invention and adoption of the lightning rod. In fact a 1782 church explosion occurred in Sumatra after the rods had been removed following someone's decision that they were more apt to attract lightning than to protect from it.

Lightning has also blown up ships at sea, the British *Resistance* being an example. This 44-gun warship went down with all hands in 1798. By 1815, 150 more cases of lightning damage to British ships were reported.

Benjamin Franklin became interested in lightning about the time that static-electricity machines were invented. This versatile genius shrewdly guessed that the electric fluid in thunderstorms was the same as that in the hand-cranked electrostatic machines. Franklin was not the first to think lightning was electricity. English scientist William Wall advanced such a theory in 1708, and so did Sir Isaac Newton.

Franklin, however, did more with his idea than the others had done. He succeeded in killing a turkey at a picnic with artificial electricity—a forerunner of electrocution as punishment for capital crimes! He also succeeded in almost killing himself several times. Electricity in the laboratory could be attracted by metal points; Franklin thought this a good test of the similarity of electricity and lightning. He devised an experiment, involving a high tower, and wrote it up in 1750 for the Royal Society. Unfortunately, there was no suitable tower in Philadelphia at that time and Franklin postponed actual testing of his hypothesis.

In France a physicist named D'Alibard beat Franklin to the punch and tried the experiment—without a tower. He simply erected a 40-foot metal mast, insulated from the ground by a bottle and supported by wooden poles and silk bindings. On May 10, 1752, an old soldier whom D'Alibard had hired—with some foresight, it would seem—held a wire connected to the ground during a thunderstorm and produced a spark from the mast.

Back in Philadelphia, Franklin was chafing because of the lack of a tower, so he too decided to go ahead without one. Not aware that the French had preceded him, he mapped out his key-and-kite approach and in June, 1752, proved that lightning was electricity, and that he was quite lucky too: In 1753 experimenter Georg Richmann was killed doing similar lightning experiments in St. Petersburg, Russia.

Franklin's kite most likely was not actually struck by lightning but simply produced a strong electrical potential from top to bottom of the string. A more daring experimenter named De Romas used copper wire on his kite, and produced a spark 9 feet long by flying the kite 600 feet high!

No less a philosopher than Immanuel Kant hailed Franklin as a "new Prometheus" who had brought down electrical fire to earth. But Franklin did not stop with merely finding out what lightning was. He built an apparatus to detect the flow of lightning in a rod he installed on his chimney. In his bedroom a wire from the rod was separated, with its ends about 6 inches apart. Franklin put a bell on the end of each half of the wire, and a brass ball was mounted on a silk thread between them. When lightning flowed through the wire the brass ball tinkled against the bells. Franklin had invented an electric chime. His real purpose was to sample the electricity produced, and he found that most of the time the lightning was negatively charged, with only an occasional positive charge detected. Franklin's lightning bells sometimes rang when there was no storm, but only a cloud over the house.

The lightning rod as a device for protecting against lightning flashes came next. He described this life- and property-saving device in *Poor Richard's Almanac* in 1753, and soon it was in use both in America and abroad. Franklin at first thought a rod might actually *prevent* the occurrence of a flash of lightning, since he had done this in the laboratory. He was thus one of the first men to work toward lightning suppression on a scientific basis. He reckoned without the tremendous power of lightning, however, and it became obvious that his rod was merely guiding safely into the earth whatever lightning it attracted.

A rival school of thought developed in England and Europe, which held that a blunt-ended rod was safer, since it would not attract lightning but merely carry it away if it occurred. To investigate this idea, one of the first large-scale studies of lightning of an artificial nature was set up in a dance hall in London. Here Benjamin Wilson, using a "cloud" 1½ feet in diameter and 155 feet long and a model building, convinced himself and those who commissioned him that bulb-shaped rods were best. Eventually it was proved, however, that pointed rods were best.

In 1764 Giovanni Bianchini wrote a scientific paper claiming that at the Castle of Duino in the Julian Alps a lance was erected with a wooden shaft as insulation, and that this lance was touched from time to time by a soldier on guard with his sword. If sparks flew it was an indication that a storm was brewing and the guard would ring a warning bell for the inhabitants, surely one of the earliest storm-warning services. The paper declared that this practice had been followed from "time immemorial," which would seem to antedate somewhat Franklin's 1752 feat.

A more modern thunderstorm warning entails picking up radio waves caused by lightning. These "wireless messages" were detected early in experiments with radio, and Marconi had to plan his first transmission across the Atlantic to guard against static caused by lightning being interpreted as a signal. Today this lightning-caused static is known as "sferics," an abbreviation of atmospherics. Such signals are reflected around the world by the atmosphere.

Another American scientific genius became interested in lightning in 1920. In that year, lightning damaged the laboratory of Charles Proteus Steinmetz and the electrical wizard subsequently did much research into the why of the phenomenon. Meantime, lightning continued to plague mankind, and even more so as civilization became more science-oriented. For example, a lightning bolt struck and destroyed the hydrogen-filled French airship *Dixmunde* in 1923. Three years later the Naval munitions depot at Picatinny Arsenal in New Jersey was struck by lightning and exploded, killing sixteen workers. This happened in spite of the lightning rods supposedly guarding the installation.

Mechanics of Lightning

A typical thunderstorm consists of one or as many as five "cells." It covers a land area of from 20 to more than 200 square miles. The base of the clouds can be from half a mile high to 2½ miles high, and thunderheads or cumulonimbus can reach 10 miles and higher. The front of the storm may extend 10 miles, and the depth ranges from 5 to 10 miles.

There are an estimated 16 million thunderstorms each year, resulting in about 100 lightning flashes each second. Depending on local terrain and atmospheric conditions, the occurrence of thunderstorms varies greatly. Java, for example, averages 322 thunderstorm days a year, while the Central Sahara Desert averages only one such day a year! North of the Arctic Circle the frequency is even less, with only one thunderstorm day every 10 years on the average. In the United States activity ranges from about 11 days a year to about 72 days a year, moving from north to south.

Lightning flashes within a cloud are more apt to occur when the distance between cloud base and ground is great. Thus over semiarid regions there is less lightning that strikes the ground than over moister areas where the cloud base is only a few thousand feet from ground level. For example, in South Africa the number of cloud flashes outnumbers cloud-to-ground lightning by ten to one, while in other areas the proportion of strokes is about equal.

Lightning strokes vary because of a cloud's charge and altitude, as well as air temperature, pressure, and resistance. "Cold" lightning is very short in duration but such high current that it has an explosive effect on what it strikes. "Hot" lightning has low currents, but lasts a longer time. It is more likely to burn its target.

Many things possess electrical charge, so it is not surprising to learn that the ionosphere, or outer atmosphere, has a strong positive charge. The earth itself is negatively charged and the difference in these charges is estimated at about 360,000 volts. A man's head is actually at a charge level of about 200 volts more positive than his feet. Moist weather may increase this difference tenfold, and a dust storm raise it to 18,000 volts! Because of this difference in electrical potential, earth is constantly losing charged particles to the atmosphere, with a leakage current of about 1,800 amperes.

Charles Augustine Coulomb showed in 1795 that the earth was leaking electricity to the sky. German physicist F. Linss estimated in 1887 that less than an hour would drain the earth. F. J. Scrase, of England's Kew Observatory, lowered this estimate to 48 minutes in 1933. Of course this does not happen, and it was suggested by C. T. R. Wilson in 1920 that thunderstorms are the means for maintaining the balance. In other words, electrons lost skyward to the pull of the positive charges in the ionosphere are replaced by electrons blasted into the earth in lightning bolts.

The thunderstorm hypothesis for maintaining the earth's leaky charge is confirmed by matching earth charge and global thunderstorm activity. Maximum storm activity occurs when the sun is shining in the afternoon on Africa and South America. Corresponding earth charge measurements were made before Wilson suggested the balance, incidentally. H. Israel of Germany has calculated 90 coulombs of current going from earth to air per square kilometer in fair weather, and 30 in precipitation. This outgo is balanced by a return to earth of 100 coulombs by "point discharge" and 20 by lightning. The oceans may add positively charged particles to the air, using a point-discharge mechanism of the waves.

The mechanism of a thunderstorm is complex and not entirely understood but a rough idea of what takes place has been reached. Within a cloud, positive and negative charges are mixed to begin with. For a lightning discharge to take place, a process called "charge separation" must take place. That is, the positives must be separated from the negatives. The forces that accomplish this separation are thought to include freezing of water droplets, the collision of droplets, the friction of wind acting on the particles, and so on. Whatever the ultimate reasons, it is an observed fact that in a developed thundercloud, which may reach 60,000 feet vertically, the ions in the top of the cloud are strongly positive and those at the bottom strongly negative.

When there is an electrical potential difference of about 10,000 volts per centimeter, there is sufficient electrical energy to create the giant spark that is the lightning bolt. This spark may jump from one cloud to another; from one part of a cloud to another part of the same cloud; or, in the case that most affects terrestrial man, from cloud to ground. Although the base of the thundercloud is negative with respect to the top, it is less negative than the earth itself. Less negative can be restated as relatively positive, and when sufficient potential builds up, lightning occurs from cloud to ground.

German scientist H. W. Dove once viewed lightning through a rotating disk with a slit in it and suggested that a lightning flash consisted of a number of strokes along the same path. A lightning stroke moves so rapidly that the human eye cannot interpret it except as a vivid flash of white that seems to jump earthward. But the invention of the Boys camera, by scientist C. V. Boys in England, gave the lightning researcher a powerful tool. This camera, with a fast-moving lens, shows the step-by-step development of the bolt, and this is far different from what we see. Ironically, Boys himself tried for thirty years and never got a satisfactory lightning picture. Sir Basil Schonland succeeded in 1933 in Africa.

General Electric

Steinmetz and an artificial lightning bolt in his General Electric laboratory.

Benjamin Franklin demonstrated the amazing insight he had into phenomena of which only the faintest actual workings could be seen. For instance, he wrote, "I am of the opinion that the stream of the electric fluid will go considerably out of a direct course for the sake of the assistance of good conductors; and that in this connection it is actually moving, though silently and imperceptibly, before the explosion, in and among the conductors." Here was a keen guess as to the existence of the "leaders" that would be detected with the Boys camera some 180 years later.

Under suitable electrical conditions, a surge of electrons from the base of a cloud moves downward toward a more negative charge at a lower level. This surge moves only about 150 feet, a millionth of a second or so, and stops as if to gather its strength. After a "lengthy" pause of some 50-millionths of a second, it repeats this downward probing surge. This is not the bolt we see, but something called a "stepped leader," a kind of reconnoitering expedition of electrons to pave the way for the main party to follow. The stepped leader averages only a few hundred miles a second.

Once the "bridge" to earth is completed, the main stroke occurs. This stroke is called a "return stroke." Following the first return stroke, there may be new downward surges of electrons, called "dart leaders," followed by secondary return strokes. Many of these pulsations have been observed in a "single" lightning flash, with each return stroke traveling at about 60,000 miles a second.

It seems fantastic that energy moving as fast as lightning does can seek out a particular path, but it can. This is why trees are poor shelters to stand under during a thunderstorm. The lightning is seeking the easiest path, and will strike an isolated tree or other object.

Fantastic amounts of energy are dissipated in lightning. Scientists have recorded individual bolts with as much as 345,000 amperes of electrical current. A current of only 1½ amperes is sufficient for house electricity, provided there is enough voltage pushing it, and lightning voltages as high as 15 million volts have been measured. A typical lightning stroke lasts less than half a second, and produces about 250 kilowatt hours of energy, enough to light a 100-watt bulb for three months. This is about $7.50 worth of electricity. A peak of 3,750 million kilowatts may be developed, however, more than the peak capacity of all electrical plants in the United States. A thunderstorm may release energy equivalent to millions of kilowatts, and a single large flash enough to operate several thousand television sets for an hour— if we could somehow convert the lightning into 110-volt electricity! Experiments along this line were made in Switzerland, where wire screens strung up in the mountains between cables trapped so much electricity that 15-foot sparks played continually about the screens.

Lightning travels along an ionized or charged path several

inches in diameter. The temperature of this "channel" may reach 30,000 degrees Centigrade. Not surprisingly such bolts can blast trees down or gouge out a hole in the earth a foot deep and 10 feet across.

Occasionally a lightning bolt produces a "fulgurite" on striking sand. This is a treelike glassy form caused by sand fusing along the red-hot path of the electrons that branch out horizontally as they reach the more conductive water-bearing soil.

Fulgurites may be more than 8 feet long, and are sometimes believed to follow the roots of bushes and plants growing in the sand, since fragments of charcoal are occasionally found on inside walls of the fulgurite. General Electric researchers have produced artificial fulgurites in the laboratory using dry sand and high-voltage electric sparks.

Australites, or tektites, strange objects from the sky, are generally thought to be from outer space or perhaps the moon. But in 1929 Chapman and Alexander theorized that they were fulgurites. In 1960, G. S. Hawkins extended this theory by suggesting that all tektites are fulgurites of fused atmospheric dust.

The sudden expansion of air caused by the great heating of the lightning creates the atmospheric shock wave we hear as thunder, to distances of 18 miles. It also seems to have an effect on precipitation. For many years, observers have talked of "rain gush" as happening right after lightning. This increased precipitation was attributed by many to the lightning. Most scientists, including meteorologist Humphreys, ridiculed the idea and said that the procedure was the reverse, and that the rain gush, caused by other factors, might be causing the lightning. Today the scientific view seems to have reverted to the earlier guess and ties the lightning and thunder to the gush. In fact, as discussed in another chapter, there are studies being conducted, particularly in Russia, on the increase in rain brought about by sound waves.

Lightning is thought to travel about 60,000 miles a second, which, while not the speed of light, is still very fast indeed. There may be flashes every 20 seconds in a thunderstorm, and although on the average only 10 bolts a year strike a square mile of area in this country, lightning can strike twice in the same place. Thus, the Empire State Building may be hit several times in a bad storm.

There are many kinds of lightning in popular discourse: for example, heat lightning, sheet lightning, and so on. There is even "ball lightning" once put down as imagined, but now becoming scientifically accepted as fact. However, it is apparently more akin to static electricity of the St. Elmo's fire type than to the bolts of lightning we are concerned with here.

Although airplanes are generally considered safe because of their metal structure, which acts as a "Faraday cage" and guides the lightning around the passengers, damage has been done to the control surfaces of aircraft. Some unexplained accidents are suspected to have been caused by the craft having been struck by lightning. Sir Basil Schonland hints that the craft may actually be triggering "disruptive" flashes that might not have occurred otherwise. This idea is based on the fact that only half the clouds through which planes were flying produced lightning prior to the bolt that struck the airplane.

Airplanes have figured importantly in lightning research. The Thunderstorm Project was launched in 1944 by the U.S. Army Air Corps, the U.S. Navy, the Weather Bureau, several airlines, and a number of educational institutions. Black Widow interceptor planes were used, with five in each mission flying at 5,000-foot-altitude increments. During 1946 and 1947, 1,363 thunderstorm flights were made by Thunderstorm Project pilots, and the craft were struck a total of 21 times by lightning. No serious damage was incurred.

Against the harm that lightning does we must balance the helpful services it performs. It equalizes the electric charge of the earth, which would otherwise leak away in short order. It also produces an estimated 100 million tons of fixed nitrogen compounds annually by breaking down the air which is oxygen and nitrogen in the ratio of about 1 part to 4. Rain deposits this nitrogen on plants where it acts as fertilizer. However, it might be possible to effect electrical charge equalization without the need for the spectacular lightning bolts. And man can produce nitrogen artificially with modest-sized sparks created in the laboratory. Let's discuss the attempts made thus far toward alleviating the damage done by lightning.

PROJECT SKYFIRE

As soon as it became apparent that man could modify precipitation with dry ice and silver iodide, scientists and others began to consider these techniques as a means of suppressing lightning as well. Each year in the United States between 10,000 and 15,000 forest fires are started by lightning. Such fires outnumber those set by man about 9 to 1. The cost of fighting them comes to an estimated $40 million, and obviously the destruction of 16 million acres of timber adds a much greater sum. In addition, many people are killed and injured in fires. For these reasons the Forest Service is understandably interested in ways of suppressing lightning, and thus reducing the toll of forest fires.

In 1952 Project Skyfire was originated at the Northern Forest Fire Laboratory, Missoula, Montana. Its goals were twofold: to gain basic knowledge of the way lightning sets forest fires, and to develop means for preventing lightning fires through weather modification. As we noted earlier, Dr. Wallace E. Howell once was credited with putting out a forest fire by causing heavy rains in the area. Sometimes nature itself deluges the fires started by lightning. However, this fire-fighting weapon cannot be counted on, particularly during "dry-lightning" storms.

For three years Donald M. Fuquay, Director of the Laboratory at Missoula, and others studied lightning-storm systems and the occurrence of lightning fires in the northern Rocky Mountains. By 1956 they were ready to begin experiments in weather modification aimed at suppressing lightning in the area. The President's Advisory Committee on Weather Control assisted, and among those who worked with Fuquay was pioneer weather maker Vincent Schaefer.

Project Skyfire field work was performed in western Montana near Missoula; in northern Idaho; and in Flagstaff, Arizona. Cloud seeding was carried out from the air, and also with the use of ground-based generators. Dry ice was used initially, and then silver iodide.

The Munitalp Foundation, a privately funded organization also worked on Project Skyfire, and among the scientists involved was Dr. Paul Macready, well known as an expert sailplane pilot in addition to his scientific pursuits.

The needed basis for the Skyfire studies was an accurate model of mountain thunderstorms. With surplus military radar, Fuquay and his colleagues established the height of cloud base and top, temperature, negative charge center of the cloud, and the time sequence in its development. A measurement system was also designed so that lightning discharges might be analyzed. Obviously one doesn't grab hold of a lightning bolt to take its pulse, but Skyfire set up a network of electrostatic field charge sensors, photocell devices for sensing luminosity, thunder transit time recorders, automatic cameras, and magnetic tape recorders. Added to the wealth of data measured with this equipment was information from a nearby Weather Bureau radar station on Point 6 Mountain.

The result of this network of measurement facilities is the ability to record each lightning bolt in the area, to tell if it is cloud-to-cloud or cloud-to-ground, to measure its intensity and duration, and to record other details of the storm generating it. For example, Fuquay counted 2,610 strokes during one year in the northern Rockies, of which 548 hit ground.

Slowly the data were pieced together. Research began to show that the most probable fire starter among the various kinds of lightning discharges is a cloud-to-ground bolt with a long continuing-current discharge. This type of lightning, called "hybrid" by the Skyfire people, begins like a typical discharge with one or more return strokes. But after its initial return stroke it goes into continuing-current discharges lasting 200 or more milliseconds. Now the problem seemed to narrow down. If this particular type of lightning discharge could be suppressed the task might be easier than that of stopping all lightning. For example, in 1957 Project Skyfire seeded on sixteen days and produced nine times as many strokes as on unseeded days. Yet there were fewer fires recorded on seeded days.

There are three electrical phenomena operating in the atmosphere: lightning discharges, point discharges, and conduction of current through the air itself. Point discharge is somewhat the reverse of Franklin's lightning rod. Blades of grass, sharp corners of sand, and other tiny projections leak electrons more readily than do flat smooth surfaces. The idea occurred to lightning-suppression experimenters to try to cause artificial "corona discharge" between many tiny conductors introduced into the thunderstorm.

Seeding to suppress lightning is thought to work in this way: an abundance of ice crystals is produced in the part of the thundercloud where most cloud-to-ground strokes of lightning are believed to originate. These ice crystals furnish additional coronal points between charge centers in the cloud. The coronal current that flows drains enough of the electricity to prevent the formation of the stepped leaders that would have otherwise formed. The additional ice crystals thus furnish an easy path for electricity and neutralize the unlike charges.

It should be pointed out that this observation is counter to one theory that says the collision of ice crystals and soft hail particles or the freezing of water drops produces the electrical charges necessary for lightning formation. However, the proof of cloud seeding is in the testing thereof, and Skyfire tests showed that in three seasons of seeding a 30 per cent reduction of cloud-to-ground lightning was recorded.

Many early amateur rainmakers apparently spoiled their chances of success by overseeding. Lightning suppression, however, seems to require so much seeding that Skyfire has never had the problem of delivering too much silver iodide to a cloud. In fact, part of the work has been directed toward development of a ram-jet type of burner that produces a much higher number of particles per volume of cloud.

Not surprisingly it was found that there is a close relationship between hail and lightning. So the two separately prosecuted modification programs are undoubtedly benefiting each other.

It is thought that most of the cloud-to-ground strokes originate in the portion of the cloud whose temperature is between minus 10 degrees Centigrade and minus 15 degrees Centigrade, and therefore the seeding plane tries to introduce its silver iodide into that portion. In 1960 and 1961 tests were conducted at Missoula using ground-based generators burning 10 kilograms (about 22 pounds) of silver iodide an hour. On seeded days, cloud-to-ground discharges were reduced 38 per cent over unseeded days. Cloud-to-cloud lightning was reduced only by 6 per cent, indicating that the experimenters were putting the seeding agents where they wanted to.

These early tests were not as conclusive as they might appear, however. Seeding was not correlated with fires started, and the possibility therefore existed that even though less lightning was produced, more of it might be of the fire-starting variety. Furthermore, tests conducted in Arizona in 1962 in which cumulonimbus clouds were seeded did not produce significant proof that cloud-to-ground lightning was reduced.

Skyfire researchers have been hampered by a shortage of funds. Because of this they are still using surplus radar gear left over from World War II, rather than newer and better equipment. Also, pilots fly light planes in and around thunderstorms, necessitating much caution and slow speed where faster, sturdier craft would make for more accurate and faster seeding. Suggested is the use of unmanned robot aircraft which could fly directly into the storm clouds with no danger to personnel.

Among those who have assisted in the Forest Service, in addition to National Science Foundation and ESSA, are the National Park Service, California State Division of Forestry, University of Montana, University of Washington, University of Arizona, and Colorado State University. Lightning-storm survey stations are located in national forests in Oregon, Washington, Montana, and in Yellowstone National Park in Wyoming.

The U.S. Army Atmospheric Sciences Laboratory at Fort Monmouth, New Jersey, has explored the possibility of pulling the teeth of the thunderstorm by dispensing "chaff" into the clouds. These bits of foil are actually tiny dipoles, short bits of metal whose ends are charged electrically opposite. Chaff is used as a radar reflector to fool receivers. As used in lightning suppression, the dipoles are intended to act as conductors for the electrical charge in clouds before it reaches a high enough potential to cause the giant spark of lightning. In actual tests chaff seeding produced strong radio noise, which is an indication of coronal activity in the thunderstorm.

Chaff tests conducted on five flights over Flagstaff, Arizona,

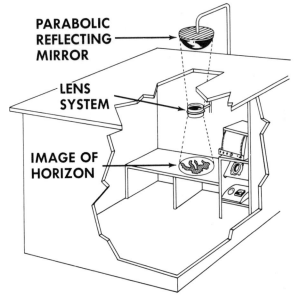

PARABOLIC REFLECTING MIRROR

LENS SYSTEM

IMAGE OF HORIZON

U.S. Forest Service

Lightning-spotting system installed in an 8-foot-square observation shelter.

resulted in a reduction of the electrical field associated with the thunderclouds in three cases. Lightning from another cloud discharged the potential of one cloud, and no change was recorded in the fifth test.

Another intriguing method of altering the lightning potential of thunderclouds is hinted in experiments by Bernard Vonnegut and C. B. Moore. These researchers charged a wire several kilometers long with 30,000 volts of electricity and thus released ions or charged particles into the atmosphere. By tracking these particles, the scientists found that the ions were carried with the air currents up to cumulus clouds. No detectable meteorological results were noted from this experiment, however, or from one in which a plane trailed a charged wire through clouds.

It is important to remember that the electrical charge of clouds affects not only lightning but precipitation as well. By proper application of electrical charges to thunderstorms it may one day be possible to eliminate not only lightning but also hail and rain if desired. A more far-fetched dream is that of somehow using the power of the lightning for industrial or utility electricity and at the same time improving our weather.

"There is no doubt that weather modification could be of enormous importance to our national defense."

—SENATOR PETER DOMINICK

8

Weather as a Weapon

FROM early times, bad weather has been classed as the enemy. Men have hurled spears at the clouds, shot arrows at thunderstorms, and fired cannon at hail. Weather and weapons have been linked another way too, with writers as long ago as Plutarch ascribing the rain to large-scale battles on the plains. Thus the soldier was not only blamed for bad weather but also furnished the weapons for trying to rout such weather.

The myth of "battle-caused weather" persists to this day, but most scientists dismiss the idea. In the realm of cold hard facts of war, however, is the obvious connection between military success and weather prevailing at battle time. Many a military commander has been beaten not by his human adversaries but by "General Mud," brought on by inopportune rain. Napoleon could beat the Russians, but not the brutal winter that froze his conquering army into a helpless rag-tag band that turned tail and fled back the way it had come, leaving casualties to the bitter cold all along the return route.

Armies on land have been bested by adverse weather, and so too have great sea armadas. In Elizabethan days furious storms at sea tore sailing ships of the line into tattered remnants and gave victory to the foe lucky enough not to be in the line of destruc-

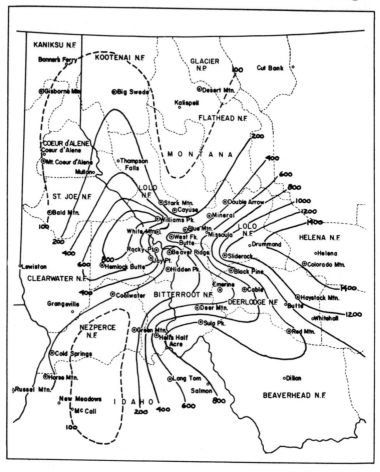

Observed cloud-to-ground discharges per 1000 square miles for July and August 1966.

tion meted out by nature on the warpath. In World War II a typhoon caught the U.S. Navy off guard and sank many of its ships with great loss of life. Here was a smashing victory for the Japanese, even more effective than had they done the sinking themselves, since they expended no effort at all in sending American craft to the bottom of the Pacific.

When men learned that firing cannon at a storm was a waste of time and gunpowder, and that they might as well shout, "Boo!" for all the good it did, they regrouped and tried to find a way to counter the losses to nature on the rampage. Weather prediction

U.S. Forest Service

Airborne seeding generator installed on light plane for Project Skyfire research.

was the answer. In offense and defense, the military made use of the technique of ballistic prediction to hit a target and to avoid being hit itself. Why not use the same tactics against General Weather? With accurate weather predictions a general could keep out of harm's way and perhaps boobytrap his opponent into getting clobbered by the weather. Scientific advisers tried to sell Abe Lincoln on using the weather militarily, but were not able to demonstrate enough accuracy.

More than a hundred years ago, a man named Francis Capen managed an interview with President Lincoln, in which he tried to sell him on the idea of weather forecasting as an aid to the Union Forces. It was the 25th of April when Capen talked with the President, and as part of his pitch he predicted rain for either April 30 or May 1. Unfortunately for Capen, it began raining on the 28th of April, and Lincoln wrote Capen that he could spare the weatherman no more of his time.

The weather makers are not yet producing a variety of weather as a new weapons system, but they are not being treated as Mr. Capen was, either. By World War II the weatherman was a key figure in battle plans. D-day was a classic example. The huge undertaking of staging the invasion of Europe hinged almost entirely on proper weather, and meteorologists came through with flying colors. Among them was Dr. Irving Krick, still engaged today in predicting weather on another front. The forces that hit France had the great advantage that weather moved from west to east, and thus they had better surveillance of conditions that would shortly influence weather in the area to be attacked. German meteorologists whose weather data was less in quantity, and later in receipt, were caught unprepared and the tide of war turned against them.

Weather prediction became a necessary and major part of military operations with World War II. But an even more remarkable innovation was introduced. For the first time, man himself changed the weather for his own military advantage. This occurred in the Battle for Britain, when the Allies successfully used the fog-dispersal system known as FIDO to permit the takeoff and landing of aircraft flights that would have otherwise been held on the ground or diverted to alternate fields or might possibly have crashed in the fog. More recently, cold fogs were dissipated in the Korean War.

It is one thing to adjust one's military actions to the weather. It is something else to adjust the weather to military actions. If man can modify the weather, he will obviously modify it for military purposes. It is no coincidence that the Army, Navy, Air Force, and Signal Corps have been deeply involved in weather modification research and development. Weather is a weapon, and the general who has control of the weather is in command over an opponent less well armed.

An article in *Fortune** stated:

Army, Navy, and Air Force are spending close to a million dollars a year on weather modification and their tremendous interest suggests that military applications extend far beyond visiting a few showers upon an enemy. It does not require a sharp mind to figure out that wartime storms might readily be infected with virulent bacteriological and radiological substances.

In the present stage of world affairs any scientific advance affecting man's ability to alter the environment has a bearing on the political relations among states and the quest for peace and security. The importance of weather modification to military operation is obvious. It would also enhance the prestige and political influence of the first country to achieve it.

Even the remote possibility that a nation might use weather modification measures to damage the economy and the civil population of another country must be recognized.

Dr. Henry G. Houghton of the M.I.T. Department of Meteorology said in 1958, "I shudder to think of the consequences of prior Russian discovery of a feasible method of weather control. An unfavorable modification of our climate in the guise of a peaceful effort to improve Russia's climate could seriously weaken our economy and our will to resist."

More recently, Dr. Edward Teller told a Senate Military Preparedness Committee that the United States could become a second-class power without war if the Russians succeed in controlling weather to produce rain over their territory and deprive America of needed rain.

While it is true that the interrelationship of weather modification around the world necessitates international cooperation, it is also true that nations historically have used whatever means came to hand to achieve a desired victory. The threat of nuclear holocaust has not stopped the production of nuclear weapons; we cannot count on weather modification escaping similar exploita-

* February, 1948, p. 109.

tion. If weather *is* to become a weapon in the arsenal of war, just how might it be used?

WEATHER WEAPONRY

Cover is a useful military device. Offensive and defensive moves are often carried out under cover of darkness. Smoke-screens are used too. Weather has also been exploited as it coincided with battle plans. A storm or fog can conceal an attack or retreat. But suppose we have the ability to create or dispel fog at will? FIDO proved two decades ago that fog could be chased. Today the techniques are more sophisticated and have proved effective in permitting aircraft flights that would not have operated if weather had been left to nature. The tactical commander's bag of tricks therefore is sure to include the creation of fog as well as its dispersal. Weather modifiers on opposing sides will fight each other's weather.

It has been suggested that submarines could carry weather control to the sea and hamper enemy fleets with fog and rain, or disperse such conditions to make the enemy craft clear-weather targets for bombing. Submarines might also create fogs and storms on an enemy coast. Weather-modifying planes could change the weather in their vicinity, and also release time-fused balloons that would drift on a precomputed path and release their material for seeding hundreds of miles "down-weather." Computer-planned operations would coordinate rain, fog, thunderstorms, hail, and clear weather with the requirements of ground and other forces in various battle areas.

With weather moving west to east, it is suggested that Russia would be at a disadvantage to the European countries. Supposedly the United States would profit from the intervening Pacific Ocean and be hampered in turn by the Atlantic that would perhaps absorb some of the changes sprayed into the atmosphere in an attempt to modify weather to the east.

The key to such weather-battles is obviously the electronic computer. Von Neumann foresaw the computer as our only hope in predicting weather or modifying it. Merely to make accurate predictions of weather in a reasonably short time will strain the capability of the next generation of computing machines. To plan a weather battle will require further great improvement in computers.

CLIMATIC WARFARE

Weather ties in with tactical warfare. Strategic warfare would involve modifying the climate affecting the enemy. In tactical modification a commander might send a storm this week to disrupt troop movements, then clear weather for two days to permit him to carry out necessary reconnaisance from the air, drop bombs, and so on. Over the long haul he might want to call down rain day in and day out for months or years in industrial areas to cause floods and discourage factory workers. At the same time, droughts would be caused by depriving the enemy's farmlands. Thunderstorms loaded with just the right kind of lightning might be created to touch off forest fires in wooded areas of the enemy land. Hail could be sent to ruin crops and even as an antipersonnel weapon. And again, the besieged nation would exert itself to counter these weather weapons with antiweather defenses.

Along with the scorched-earth attack a commander might scorch the earth more literally with huge plastic focusing reflectors placed in space above the enemy's land. These would concentrate the sun's rays and create killing heat in selected areas. Or permanent high-altitude clouds might be formed that would lower temperatures to create a similarly harmful effect on the enemy. Added to such science-fiction horror stories are suggestions of flooding the enemy by melting the polar caps, using techniques discussed in an earlier chapter.

In a 1966 Congressional hearing on weather modification Senator Cannon said: "Successful weather modification could be an important detail in our national defense posture." Other legislators, and some scientists as well, voiced similar opinions.

Answers of the military to questions on use of weather as a weapon vary from noncommittal evasion to frank admissions. Dr.

Chalmers W. Sherwin of the Department of Defense responded to a question from Senator Peter Dominick as to the significance of weather as a weapon in these words:

I believe that I can state with assurance that at the present state of confidence and knowledge, it has no direct military weapon type of activity value. The ability to control warm fog for landings is very important. . . . The ability to produce clouds could have direct military utility and in that sense would be a component of a weapons system.

Dr. Pierre St. Amand, doing weather modification research for the U.S. Navy, said of it:

Primarily the work is aimed at giving the U.S. Navy and the other armed forces, if they should care to use it, the capability of modifying the environment, to their own advantage or to the disadvantage of an enemy. We regard the weather as a weapon. Anything one can use to get his way is a weapon and the weather is as good a one as any.

As yet we have no formal Tactical Weather Command or Strategic Climate Corps. The idea of clobbering an enemy with a blizzard or starving him with an artificial drought still sounds like science fiction. But so did talk of atom bombs before 1945. Weather is inevitably a weapon; the most we can hope for is that it will always be used in the war *against* hunger and flood instead of to cause such catastrophes.

"Clearly life and climate interact on each other."

—HARLOW SHAPLEY, Astronomer

9

Changing the Climate

IT is one thing to dream of making it rain in a localized area, to prevent a storm, or to chase a bank of fog. But what of actually altering the *climate* of a region? Having barely succeeded with weather making it would seem rash to talk seriously of climate changing. Yet, with his ample supply of nerve to dare the impossible, man is close to beginning experiments in the modification of the climate he lives in. Universal Chamber of Commerce weather is not right around the corner, and winter snows and summer heat waves will be with us for a long time yet. But if it is humanly possible, the weather changer will change the climate too.

We have seen that a number of factors are involved in climatic conditions on earth. Included are the sun's radiation; the capacity and conductivity of earth's crust; the atmosphere; the phase changes of moisture: ice, water, and vapor; photochemical reactions such as those taking place in plants; volcanic activity; and radioactivity in the earth.

Obviously there are several ways in which the heat budget of earth, and consequently its weather and climate, could be changed. Changes in the energy emitted from the sun; changes in that energy between sun and earth's atmosphere; changes in the atmosphere itself, including magnetic fields; and finally changes in the albedo or reflecting quality of earth.

The report, "Weather and Climate Modification Problems and Prospects," published in 1966 by the National Academy of Sciences–National Research Council, has this to say in its introduction:

All atmospheric processes and weather phenomena are ultimately induced by the solar energy reaching the earth. *At present,* we cannot modify that energy at its source, nor can we intervene between the sun and the earth's atmosphere. . . .

The italics have been added, since the qualifying phrase seems to imply that at some future date man may be able to modify the sun's energy. However, such intervention at nature's power plant itself seems still far in the future. If man intends to change climate today he must do so in other ways.

In 1862 Henry Adams wrote:

Not only shall we be able to cruise in space, but I see no reason why some future generation wouldn't give it [the earth] another rotary motion so that every zone would receive in turn its due portion of light.

Man is not yet able to juggle the earth about on its axis, although science-fiction writers have done so for years and pseudoscience writers have suggested that ice ages came when the earth tumbled in its spinning, like a top run down.

By turning earth into a spaceship, man *might* succeed in tipping the earth's axis farther from the vertical, or perhaps in straightening it up. The orbit about the sun might be made more circular or more elongated; brought nearer to or farther from the sun. Stopping the rotation of earth, slowing, or reversing it, would likewise have a great effect on weather and climate.

Unable to tamper grossly with the sun or the earth, for the moment, at least, man is constrained to change climate by more modest means. But inherently he does have the ability to do so, as pointed out by astronomer Harlow Shapley:

Although climate is chiefly a matter of winds, ocean currents, sunshine, rains, and snow, it involves also the responses of plants and animals to these physical factors. What plants grow on the mountain sides and control the evaporation? What animal affects the weather by meddling with the water courses, thereby producing lush vegetation in arid regions? *Clearly life and climate interact on each other.* If life had never appeared on the earth's surface, the local climates would have been different from those which have prevailed. And if the climate had everywhere been unchanging throughout geologic time, the varied life we know—the millions of species—might not have come about: possibly the organisms would never have got their start in the dim Pre-Cambrian ooze.*

The italics have been added to emphasize a key point. Shapley is saying that climate has evolved, perhaps concurrently with life. Life is part of climatological evolution, and recently man—and his blossoming technology—has become an active factor in the process. Before proceeding further, we should mention the matter of scale—the scope of climate modification effected by man.

Like weather, climate is considered on three typical modification scales. These are *microclimate,* up to about 9 miles in horizontal dimensions, *mesoclimate,* from 9 to 120 miles, and *macroclimate,* more than 120 miles. Man has made some microclimate progress with such basic developments as clothing and shelter, heating and air conditioning, greenhouses for plants, smudgepots and other heating devices, shades, and covering devices. Mesoscale changes have been effected through elimination of forests, temperature and wind changes caused by city growth, and changes caused by irrigation and other aspects of large-scale farming. Man-made erosion has changed climate, perhaps even on the macroscale level.

As with modification of weather, modifying climate presupposes some understanding of what makes climate. For example, the man who would cause the winds to cease might well learn why they blow in the first place. Hadley, who in 1735 published his paper explaining the mechanics of the trade winds, laid the groundwork for such understanding. Although much is yet to be learned, one thing climatologists do know is that climate in one area or region is intimately connected with that elsewhere.

* Harlow Shapley, *Climatic Change* (Cambridge: Harvard University Press, 1953), p. 1.

Changing the wind pattern over a desert implies doing something to conditions elsewhere. Creating a rain belt in one place may well rob moisture from a region "downwind" of the first.

Atmospheric Control

Although man cannot yet intervene between the sun and the atmosphere, within the atmosphere itself he has long done so, as we shall see in the chapter on accidental modification of climate. By pumping billions of tons of carbon dioxide into the atmosphere he has accounted for perhaps 15 per cent of that gas now present. The result, according to some scientists, is a barely perceptible rise in the temperature of the earth. Continuing to smog up the air at present rates will increase the carbon dioxide content by 50 per cent in another twenty years, with an appreciable increase of temperature, melting of the icecaps, and so on.

If man can do this much without even trying, how successful will he be if and when he *deliberately* sets out to change the content of our atmosphere? Science-fiction tales have described making other planets in the solar system habitable by releasing carbon dioxide into the atmosphere to retain more heat. We might do this on earth, or *reduce* the carbon dioxide content to cool things down.

The explosion of nuclear bombs in the atmosphere has resulted in another material added to the atmosphere. Dr. Edward Teller has said that if we were to explode a hundred nuclear bombs per year for a twenty-year period we might so lower the temperature by blocking out radiation that a new ice age would be created.

As yet we have not engaged in a climate-modification program as such which involves changing the atmosphere, although we well might before too long. We are beginning to experiment with other means of altering weather on a long-range basis. However, this includes such techniques as changing the albedo, or reflectance, of the land surface and also that of water.

Surface Changes

Some years ago the Russians reported success with a program of melting snow much faster than it would by itself, and thus increasing the growing season for wheat and other crops. This melting was accomplished by simply "painting" the snow black. Lampblack was dusted over the snow, and caused it to absorb more heat and thus melt more quickly. The reflection quality of snow is obviously quite high, as anyone who has lived in snowy regions knows, and requires glasses or squinted eyes for protection.

Fine as the idea sounds, blacking the frozen north to warm it may prove to be a project beyond the scope even of tomorrow's technology. Fresh snow would obliterate the black heat trap effectively; winds could blow it away. Just laying down such a cover is a tremendous project. To spread a film of carbon black just 4/1000 inch thick from the North Pole down to 65 North Latitude would require 1½ billion tons of the stuff! Using cargo planes with a capacity of 10 tons each would still require 150 million flights to get the job done. As one scientist dryly remarked, "This would take considerable time."

A more elegant suggestion for warming the polar areas is that of maintaining cloud cover over frozen seas. During the long polar night this would retain more heat in the atmosphere below, and on the surface as well. Just how this cloud cover would be provided and kept in place has not been solved as yet, although it might seem within the grasp of the artificial rainmakers. Another approach suggested is to add quantities of carbon dioxide to the atmosphere, and this gas would also hold heat below it.

Changing the surface of earth can be done in other ways. It has been argued that deforestation has altered climate in some areas. Temperature variations do increase when an area is denuded of trees, there is a faster runoff and increased evaporation of water, and an increase in wind speeds at the surface. Some climatologists have made a career of preaching the benefits of reforestation. Whether or not there actually is increased rainfall in such areas is a contested point, but the replacement of trees may reverse the processes attributed to deforestation.

Aerodynamic surface roughness is important in microclimate. For instance, the air temperature at a height of a few feet can be cooler by 1 or 2 degrees Fahrenheit over a hot airport runway than over the cooler grass areas surrounding it. Aluminum foil can be used to reflect heat, black plastic can absorb as much as 90 per cent of it. However, it should be remembered that darkening the earth's surface might lead to side effects not desired. For example, if it caused additional cloud cover there would be less heat striking it and thus the purpose of the coating would be defeated.

The trade winds in the West Indies blow air over the island of Anegada, which is about 20 square miles, a relatively small area. Even during the dry season, the warming effect of this island produces a cloud "street" some 20 miles long and up to 6,000 feet thick. As a result rainfall occurs. Satellite photographs have shown longer and thicker island clouds to be quite common during the wet season. Dr. Joanne Malkus Simpson believes that since asphalt has twice the heat advantage of the natural soil on Anegada, the use of man-made cloud streets to produce rain should be investigated.

Conversely, it is suggested that increasing the albedo of certain areas, rather than decreasing it with blacking, might also effect long-range changes in atmospheric conditions. In the extremely dry desert region of south Peru the heated sand on an upslope results not in rainclouds, but in the dry air characteristic of a desert. This phenomenon is caused by a particular set of conditions. The solution would be to increase the albedo of the slope so that it will reflect more heat away, or to moisten the slope by irrigation.

Scientists studying the Rajputana desert area in Pakistan and India believe that it is actually a man-made desert, caused by dust in the air. This caused "infra-red cooling" of the air, inhibiting natural convection and rainfall. The scientists propose to stabilize the surface of the land area so that more dust will not be added to the lower 10,000 feet of the atmosphere. The addition of a grass cover by irrigation should result in a halt in the desert's slow march at the rate of about half a mile a year, and eventually bring wet enough weather back to sustain the vegetation and change the desert into arable land.

Because winds are important in climate, suggestions have been made for intentionally altering the pattern and velocity of surface winds. One scheme would coat the ocean with a thin film of oil to reduce its surface friction. Another would plaster the Great Plains region of the United States with billboards to slow down surface winds and prevent the carrying away of soil. The beauty of this scheme is that private advertisers would foot the bills for the climate modification! There are obviously drawbacks to this proposal. The highway-beautification program would surely frown on such a cluttering of the landscape, and there are hardly enough residents or motorists to justify the kind of billboard jungle necessary to produce the desired effect.

OCEANS

If snow can be melted artificially, what about ice? Again the Russians have ideas on the subject, and melting the ice of the frozen Arctic Sea is a pet project of theirs. Such schemes fill many scientists with horror at the thought of possible side effects created by melting billions of tons of ice. Cautionary tales are told of the oceans rising 40 feet around the world, and New York and other port cities being submerged while Siberia basks in new warmth. Russia has seaports too, and some Russian scientists claim to have delved deep into the probable results and decided that flooding would not be the case.

More than ten years ago Russian scientists seriously proposed another project for warming the northern reaches of the planet. Involved in this scheme would be the damming of the Bering Strait so that cold Arctic water would be blocked from the warm Pacific. The object obviously was to give a better climate to Siberia. Russia would gain ice-free ports on the Pacific the year round, and agriculture too would benefit. The geographical limits of crop raising would be pushed farther northward, and land already cultivated would be much warmer and permit a longer growing season.

This plan raised scientific hackles around the world and in the popular press when it was first broached. It was immediately pointed out that the Bering Dam would most likely cause more Arctic water to flow across the top of North America. This would augment the already icy Labrador Current flowing down Davis Inlet along the Maritimes coast of eastern Canada. Farming in the Maritimes would suffer from worse storms and earlier frost. In addition, the port of Halifax might be closed in winter.

The Arctic Sea accounts for about 3 per cent of the earth's heat budget, Russian investigators say. Increasing its heat intake 50 per cent by melting the ice so that the water would soak up more of the sun's rays would add only about 1½ per cent to the total amount of heat available to earth. Furthermore, most of the ice to be melted is already below the water, and ice loses part of its volume as it melts anyway. Therefore, according to the Russian researchers, there would be no harmful effects to other bodies of water.

In the ensuing years it developed that the plan was not as simple as some fearfully assumed. Russian scientists pointed out that the idea was not just to keep Arctic waters out of the Pacific, but to mix Atlantic warm water with the Arctic and warm it up. Another report, attributed to Russian scientist Arkady Borishovich, suggested that in addition to the Bering Dam the Russians would install hundreds of nuclear-powered stations to pump in warm Pacific water. This would be robbing somebody of warm water, however, and prompted more shouts of alarm.

In a paper entitled "Climatic Change and Climate Control," Russian scientist M. I. Budyko in 1962 wrote that removing the Arctic ice pack would result in summer temperatures of 10 to 20 degrees Centigrade (50 to 68 degrees Fahrenheit), and winter temperatures of 5 to 10 degrees Centigrade (41 to 50 degrees Fahrenheit). F. I. Badgley in 1961 reached the conclusion that permanent melting of the Arctic would never be achieved, but in his paper Budyko suggested that the cover, once removed, would not re-form.

It was suggested that in self-defense the West would have to install a series of atomic heating plants in the Arctic to warm its waters and maintain the climate of areas otherwise harmfully affected. The trouble with this admittedly costly solution was that it would probably hasten the melting of the ice of Greenland's mountains—some 140,000 cubic miles of the stuff. An appreciable production of water from such melting could raise the world's oceans 5 feet according to some estimates, and even five more feet of water would flood much of the Netherlands, as well as cities like New York and London, and hundreds of other cities smaller but no less important to their inhabitants. Solution to this impasse, offered tongue-in-cheek, was to air-condition Greenland with nuclear power.

It is conceivable that nuclear energy might be used to warm the seas. Electricity requires a more complex power plant than does simple heat, and a nuclear furnace is a relatively easy proposition. Detonating an H-bomb under water has been suggested as a means of producing fresh water at sea. The same technique might also be used to warm the sea and be less complicated than setting up nuclear-powered pumps to do the job by mechanical mixing that also steals heat from another water source.

As meteorologist Captain Howard T. Orville put it a decade ago, damming the Bering Strait is more than a weekend project, and as yet Russia has made no concrete strides in this direction. However, Orville did point out that the Russians had completed some sizable reclamation efforts, including creation of a 100-mile-long artificial sea of Tsymlyanskaya as a link between the Don and Volga rivers.

An even bigger project once considered by the Russians was the damming of the Ob and Yenisey rivers, both of which flow into the Arctic. The resulting inland sea in Siberia was to provide a more moist and moderate climate as winds blew over it to the dry frigid steppes. Three other northern Russian rivers were also considered in such vast reclimatization projects. These were the Pechora, Vychegda, and Sukhona, west of the Ural Mountains. The impounded waters from three rivers would be carried by canal to the Kama and the Volga rivers, and into the Caspian Sea. Here again the idea was creation of a large body of water to modify the climate of the surrounding area.

An important consideration with regard to plans to warm up Siberia is that the "Siberian high" is a powerful influence on weather to the east. The area is one of the coldest in the world, and it is the weather factory for winds that start China's monsoons. It may also affect the weather in California, New York, and London. Thus, by modifying the Siberian high to their own benefit, the Russians would also be changing weather most of the way around the world, not necessarily for the good of others.

It would be wrong to assume that the earth is allotted only so much "good weather," and that improving it one place automatically hurts conditions elsewhere. It may eventually be possible to improve everyone's weather, but the point to remember is that John Donne's pronouncement applies to climate as well as to man. No climate is an island unto itself; all climates stem from other climates, and affect other climates. An example of this on a microclimate scale occurs when too many people use heat pumps that tap a river or ground water as a reservoir of heat or cold, and thus depreciate the water's value for other uses.

The notion of improving regional climate by addition of a large body of water is subject to some qualifying facts of atmospheric or meteorological life. It is not practical in every case to add a large body of water to an area as a climate modifier. This approach was suggested for arid Arizona until a meteorologist, Dr. James McDonald of the University of Arizona, sat down and worked out how large a body would be required: something the combined size of Lakes Erie and Ontario was needed to have a marked effect on climate!

Increase of Arizona summer rains by 10 per cent would require the addition of 20,000 square miles of lake. And the belief that this artificially added water would stay in the region and become a permanent part of the water budget is unfounded. This belief hinges on the theory that a given molecule of water will be involved in many successive hydrologic cycles. Experiments show that this is not the case, however, and that only one such cycle occurs on the average, even over a large area. This is because the time factor for the cycle is something like ten days, in which time even a mild 10-mile wind would have carried the molecule some 2,400 miles east. The Arizona artificial lake (dubbed "Lake Fallacy" by McDonald) would eventually be precipitated in the Atlantic Ocean and could not survive without constant replacement from some other source.

Just as men have suggested altering the surface of snow and ice to effect climate changes, they have come up with ideas for changing the surface of the sea for various reasons. Dr. Irving Langmuir, who pioneered weather modification, earlier suggested the use of a monomolecular film spread on water to retard evaporation. Such coatings are now being applied and show that moisture loss can be cut as much as 60 per cent. Despite many shortcomings, such as loss of the protective film because of wind, boat wakes, and so on, it is obvious that water is retained that otherwise would escape to the atmosphere.

While man saves water for his reservoirs, what does he do to the air downwind of the body of water? Evaporation of water cools the air and adds moisture to it. A plastic film over the water will result in warm dry air over it. And the water itself will be heated. Thus there are side effects that must be carefully considered before large-scale attempts are made to change nature's plan.

Russia has made bolder plans for climate modification, but she has no corner on the market. For example, it has been proposed that a dam be built at Gibraltar. As the level of the Mediterranean Sea rose, it might be possible to desalt water and irrigate the Sahara, not quite as direct a means of modifying climate in surrounding areas as the Russians propose, but climate modification nonetheless.

TIMETABLE FOR CLIMATE CHANGING

Man has been very successful in modifying microclimates ranging in size from the skindiver's wet suit to the enclosed baseball stadium of the Houston Astros. In Arizona and elsewhere, air conditioning has moved from rooms, to homes, to automobiles and buses, to large buildings and even to outdoor malls. Orchards and other agricultural areas are warmed and provided with desirable wind currents or calm air in a number of ways.

The size of modified climates is growing. Enclosed cities, tented with clear plastic, may one day provide temperate climate the year round, learning something perhaps from exploration of the moon which seems destined to begin soon. It is suggested that sheets of plastic placed some distance beneath the surface of the sea may have large-scale effects on temperature and evaporation. More startling schemes involve the orbiting in space of huge plastic reflectors to warm up certain areas of earth, such as ice-bound lakes or canals. Artificial suns are suggested to light up the sky at night and also to furnish heat to warm cold areas.

A recent article in a scientific journal suggests the foreseeable limits of such climate modification as about 10,000 square miles. This is an area 100 miles on a side, huge in contrast to an air-conditioned home. However, when compared with the entire earth it is tiny, since the latter is some 200 million square miles in area.

Modification of climate on the microscale, and even on the mesoscale, has been demonstrated to be possible by cloud seeding and other experiments. Macroscale modification, on the other hand, would require so much greater an expenditure of energy and material that most meteorologists feel that it remains entirely theoretical, in spite of Dr. Langmuir's claims to the contrary following his cloud-seeding experiments in New Mexico.

The National Academy of Sciences (NAS) had this to say in 1966 about climate modification:

Today's need for improved hypotheses of climatic change stems from the fact that human activities have reached the stage at which they can effect significant changes in global environmental parameters. Because of the spectacular rate of growth of human influence on the environment, for good or bad, a new urgency is attached to climatic history and theory. However, geological and paleontological considerations and simple intuition may not yield enough in themselves, for ancient evidence is incomplete and ambiguous. Questions concerning the general circulation of the atmosphere, land-ocean-atmosphere interactions, and details of the earth-system's use and disposal and solar energy all have to be collectively answered in the course of developing a comprehensive geodynamical model with which we can perfect theories and test hypotheses of climatic change.

The NAS report points out that only on a local scale have experiments in weather and climate modification been actually carried out. Modification of the *general* circulation system has not been attempted because of the stupendous energy and logistic effort that would be required. Thus our ideas of large-scale climate modification are based totally on theories. Until we have better understanding of the causes we will not be able to modify the climate usefully on a very large scope.

Ability to forecast accurately is a requisite to controlling weather or climate accurately. It is hoped that improvements in knowledge of circulation systems, plus the ability to release large amounts of energy, will result in man's being able to trigger those changes he desires by introducing energy at the right time and the right place. As the NAS report adds:

It is becoming apparent that our understanding is now virtually good enough to permit us to predict reliably the qualitative influence of certain kinds of massive tampering—for example, removal of the Rocky Mountains, or a twofold alteration in the earth's roughness, or a 20-percent change in the atmosphere's CO_2. However, if we look for the effect of subtle changes, more accessible to human intervention, then our understanding and our ability to simulate natural phenomenon will have to be much greater.

Man is closer to leveling the Rockies than he is to altering earth's orbit, but not close enough that the former technique is yet available. The same applies to roughening up the earth's surface sufficiently to make great changes in wind patterns, and to adding 20 per cent more carbon dioxide in something less than years.

The possibility of using relatively small "triggering impulses" to nudge weather and climate into large-scale changes has been suggested. Just as a tiny bit of carbon dioxide or silver iodide introduced when conditions are right can produce a result far outweighing the actual energy in the seeding process, so might a precisely timed and gauged impulse swing macroscale weather and climate into a different course. Langmuir felt that he was

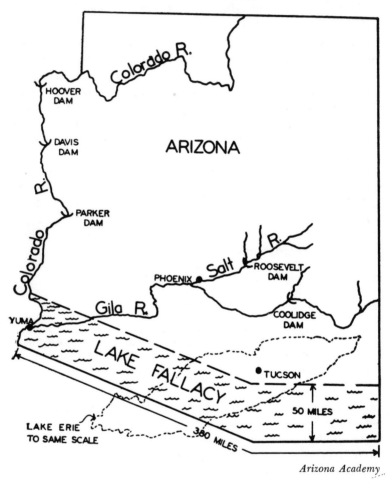

To produce a 10 per cent increase in July rainfall over Arizona would call for creation of the 19,000-square-mile "Lake Fallacy" shown above. The comparative size of Lake Erie is indicated by the dashed outline, drawn to the same scale.

periodically triggering the weather, and the feeling today is that this approach may be realized—if we can learn enough about the weather to know what such triggers actually do to circulation patterns.

Success here could mean such things as the elimination of hurricanes while maintaining sufficient movement of heat toward the poles to prevent some other manifestation of weather or climate on a large scale. Such climatic results as arid deserts might also be eliminated without disrupting beneficial climate elsewhere. Man might even prevent the recurrence of ice ages through skillfully controlled application of triggering pulses of energy at the right time and place.

Again, we should keep a clear distinction between climate and weather. O. Henry remarked that "we may achieve climate but the weather is thrust upon us." We should also remember that bad as the climate strikes us now, it could be worse because it has been in the past. Climatic conditions may get worse in the future, and man himself may be to blame. Climate modification, then, is a more serious venture to be embarked on, with ramifications so far-reaching that a new generation of computers will be needed before we can safely proceed.

"No accidents are so unlucky but that the wise may draw some advantage from them; nor are there any so lucky but that the foolish may turn them to their own prejudice."

—LA ROCHEFOUCAULD

10

Modification by Accident

MAN has *consciously* sought to change his environment for several centuries, with success ranging from excellent to trivial. The trivial success has occurred in his attempts to change weather on a larger than "microclimate" scale. Paradoxically, he has achieved greater success in modifying the weather inadvertently: *unconsciously* man has been affecting his environment from the day he appeared in it.

The sad condition of our waterways is common knowledge today; it is well said that had we intended to pollute them we could hardly have done a better job. In like manner we are accidentally altering our atmospheric environment. In a study of the possibility of intentionally changing weather, it is well to see how much man has accomplished in this direction quite by happenstance.

For a long time there have been those who suggested that man was modifying the weather inadvertently. An early claim was that deforestation had reduced precipitation, and there have been some remarkable cart-before-the-horse "proofs" given for this charge. For example, there are great forests in the wet northwest part of the United States, while none grow in the deserts. Therefore, forests produce rain!

This is no new concept, and is expressed in an old poem that describes:

> Afric's barren sand,
> Where nought can grow because it raineth not,
> And where no rain can fall to bless the land
> Because nought groweth there.

Here seemed a vicious circle of drought caused by man in denuding the land of trees and vegetation. In the 1930's President Franklin D. Roosevelt's "Shelter Belt" program to plant thousands of trees in the drought-stricken Midwest was an attempt to apply this idea of reversing the dry cycle by intervening with forests to create rain.

Other agents, before and since, have been blamed for the lack of rain. Military operations, as we have seen, were believed to induce rain as an incidental by-product. War led to the "scorched-earth" policy as early as the days of the Scythians retreating from the army of Darius; thus if the deforestation theory had been right war might well have been guilty of terminating rainfall. Later, when gunpowder superseded the lance and sword, it was held that these chemicals injected into the air caused rain to come. Wiser heads have suggested that wars or battles generally were fought in good weather, and that good weather is inevitably followed sooner or later by bad weather.

Dr. Langmuir noted a weekly cycle in rainfall during his seeding experiments in New Mexico, and suggested it might reflect the human seven-day routine. This was no new idea, and as early as 1929 researcher J. R. Ashworth felt there was some evidence that rainfall was less in the manufacturing town of Rochdale, England, on Sunday, the day the mills were closed.

Later, radio, of all things, was blamed for chasing rain! In the 1930's pleas were made to stop broadcasting from midwestern stations during the drought, because many thought the "electrified air" was stopping rain from falling. And of course the atom bomb provided another scapegoat for those who considered science the interloper upsetting the weather picture.

Wrong as many of our ideas are about man as a bungling accidental rainmaker or rain-killer, it is all too true that there is much evidence to support the basic idea itself. Unwittingly we *have been* doing something about the weather, and for a long time.

Man: The Weathermaker

It may be pointed out that when a striding man pushes himself ahead a step, he also pushes the world back a bit. Considering the masses involved, earth is much less affected by man than man is by earth in this case. Yet even in the matter of climate man has been making his relative mark. Before he does anything else, man inhales the air of his environment. The air he breathes out is not of the same composition, having lost in oxygen and gained in carbon dioxide in the encounter with human lungs. To be sure, all our present bulging population puffing rapidly has not sufficient combined lung volume to affect greatly the average oxygen content of the layer of air that surrounds earth. Additionally, living plants enter the atmospheric cycle and convert carbon dioxide back to oxygen for man's reuse. But the principle is obvious and basic: by the mere involuntary act of breathing, man alters his atmospheric environment. This fact is pointed up sharply when a human is trapped in a closed container such as a submarine or an icebox. Very quickly he alters the air surrounding him so that it is no longer capable of sustaining him. By his very nature, then, man is incapable of *not* changing his environment.

Breathing, in addition to providing man with the oxygen he needs for muscle power, also allows him the power of speech. Speech, tools, and fire have been called the tripod of culture and each of these three underpinnings has had its effect on man's environment. Since talk began, surely, man has talked about the weather, damning or praising it as he happened to be soldier or farmer, lover or poet. In time speech would lead to science and science to sophisticated methods of modifying weather and climate. But long ago, even man's lesser tools began to do this. And far before he built his first dam or dug his first irrigation ditch, man used fire to change his environment.

Antedating man's first blackening of forest and sky, natural fire in several forms caused great conflagrations with resultant changes in weather. Much of nature is electrical, and early in earth's growth furious bolts of this spectacular energy must have set devastating fires. Volcanoes spewed forth ash and molten lava, which burned all the vegetation it contacted and some that it merely approached. From natural sources Prometheus stole fire and put it to his own uses. With fire man desolated vast forest areas and choked the skies. Perhaps rainfall was affected directly by these phenomena, and the early rainmaker's reliance on fire for performing his magic may be based on such observations. Just as probably, deforestation had a long-range effect on climate. Lack of trees speeded surface winds and changed the temperature of the ground as well as its moisture content. Although scientists today do not agree that deforestation has had the effect generally and historically ascribed to it, there seems some interrelationship between denuded areas and rainfall, floods, temperature, and winds.

The Indonesian volcano, Krakatoa, in 1883 erupted a cubic mile of rock and poured thousands of tons of volcanic ash into the upper reaches of the atmosphere. For several years this veil blocked sunlight and actually made a slight change in the temperature. Before too long man would duplicate Krakatoa with his own outpouring of contaminants from fires and other more sophisticated forms of combustion, principally those of his factories and automobile engines.

Floods and droughts prompted man to do something to stabilize his water supply. Tools let him build dams and dig ditches and thus change the old waterways that nature had provided. It is doubtful that early man greatly modified his environment, and yet legends tell of great lush oases and even lake regions in Africa that today are desert. New surveys are finding great quantities of water below these deserts, giving rise to the intriguing question of whether primitive farmers and water engineers or other environment changers did indeed do something to cause a change in their land. What of today's engineers armed with modern earth-moving equipment up to and including the hydrogen bomb?

When the first pictures of the planet Mars came back devoid of any evidences of man-made improvements on that dry world, it was correctly pointed out that photos taken of our own planet from a like altitude were similarly uncommunicative about what was really down here. From a hundred miles above the earth there is no evidence, during daylight hours, of the fantastic complex of civilization that is so painfully obvious to those of us driving the freeways or walking the canyons of a big city. There is a lesson here for those who are not aware of, or who have not kept in proper perspective, the workings of man as compared in size with those of nature that produced him.

A flying saucer orbiting earth at altitude would be no more aware of man today than the day the first human drew breath and began to produce an ecological feedback to his atmosphere. How can man, such a tiny speck on the geological scale, be expected to have any effect on earth's weather or climate? But then, how can a gene be expected to have been a factor in, say, the Empire State Building or Grand Coulee Dam?

Individually man has little effect on his surroundings, but put him in close company with another hundred thousand or so of his fellows and the picture changes. True, the being in the flying saucer would still not have been aware of us a couple of centuries back when cities of such size began to grow up. Yet its computer-analyzed weather data would have begun to print out the inescapable fact that the weather around cities was changing even though man was not consciously trying to change it. Actually, the changes were generally not those he would have wanted anyhow.

Scientists have turned up evidence of an "ecology of fire," in which accidental fires from lightning or other natural causes actually benefited the life forms. Man's intervention, in the form of fire control, thus forces changes on the environment and resultant changes in the ecology of an area.

Heat is the prime mover for weather. Heat causes the evaporation of water, the circulation of air masses. Some of the sun's heat is trapped in vegetation and thus taken out of circulation. But fire puts some of this heat back into the weather factory. Man has burned for agriculture, for hunting, for military "scorched-earth" policies these thousands of years and has thus, unknown to himself, been a thermal factor in the weather.

Agriculture

Diversion of waterways has been done primarily for the benefit of agriculture; agriculture consumes many times as much water as does domestic use. Since water is a primary factor in weather, waterworks obviously affect the weather. But other aspects of farming also have their effects. The dust storms that plagued America in the 1930's are an example. Presumably man himself was at least partly to blame for this catastrophe because of overgrazing of grasslands. Unable to hold the soil, the region became the Dust Bowl of the nation, and black clouds of the stuff darkened not only the Midwest but wafted all the way to the east coast. What effect does such contamination of the atmosphere have on weather?

The albedo, or reflectance of the earth's surface, is a factor in weather. So too is the roughness of the land. Farmland is generally level and smooth, and crops affect the albedo. Often the effect is limited and noticed in only a small area, however.

In Arizona, as in other irrigated areas, one standard comment on the weather is that it is much more moist now than it was before the canals went into operation. It is difficult to convince an old-timer who believes this, but the weight of scientific evidence argues otherwise. Evaporating water from the irrigation does raise the humidity, but this effect is of a local nature. Studies near Yuma, for example, showed that the air a few feet above a 100,000-acre project had a higher humidity than the ambient or surrounding reading, but 12 feet above the ground the humidity was normal, and even downwind of the irrigation project ambient humidity prevailed only 100 feet from the borders of the field. Similar studies in Phoenix and Tucson indicate that the moistening effect of irrigation is local and does not have the far-reaching effect that pioneers attribute to it.

CITIES

Any human dwelling or collection of dwellings has some slight effect on the microclimate surrounding it. In hot climates we produce cool weather inside our homes with refrigeration; in cold climates we accomplish the reverse by heating. There are also other inescapable changes in the microclimate surrounding a city, and for a number of reasons.

As might be expected, wind speeds tend to drop in the environs of a city. Buildings and other structures offer resistance and extract kinetic energy from the moving air, thus slowing it down. The reflectance of a city is generally different from the surrounding natural countryside; mostly it is less. Thus the city is hotter than the surrounding country, as glider pilots and other fliers know from the "thermals," or rising air currents, they encounter over them. A figure of 10 degrees Centigrade has been given as typical for the temperature difference from city to surrounding country. Of course all the extra heat does not come from additionally trapped solar heat. Man burns fuel in cities to run power plants, warm his home, cook his food, operate his car, and so on. And as we have seen, heat is a motive force in the weather machinery.

Might we not also expect other weather and climate changes? Weather records for growing towns indicate rainfall increase of as much as 10 per cent within two decades, relative to the surrounding country. Snow has been observed over heavily industrialized areas when none fell in areas around the town or city.

An example of the amount of heat a city can produce is evident in studies of Vienna reported in 1956. The heat from coal-burning furnaces and electrical power was about half that received from the sun during the wintertime. People themselves can produce a fair amount of heat: several thousand kilogram-calories per person per day. When thousands of people jam into a stadium the combined heat output is enough to raise the temperature in the vicinity measurably.

Although more far-reaching than the irrigation humidity effects previously described, these city-induced changes in weather and climate are still fairly well localized as far as is known. A few miles away from the city the weather is perhaps little affected by the fact of wind or temperature difference within the city.

Alterations of wind patterns and temperature are enough to modify the weather and climate of cities, but neither of these factors is as potent and dangerous as another. This third output of civilization is largely a by-product of fire—the black blot of smog that darkens many of the world's cities and has killed as many as 2,000 in a single tragedy.

Smog

Much has been written about smog and its deadly effects on our civilization. We shall concern ourselves here with a different aspect of smog—its effect on the weather and the climate.

A single cigarette, or even a fireplace or the exhaust of a truck, has little effect on the sea of atmosphere. Nature quickly purifies the air, much as it does water that is fouled. But there are limits to this healing of our atmosphere and in many many places we have far exceeded these limits. By the early 1950's, for example, it was estimated that the city of Los Angeles was spewing some 50,000 tons of combustion products into the air *each day*. The most obvious results of this dirtying of the atmosphere are the disappearance of legendary California sunshine from the area a good part of the year, the eye-burning sensation, and the hazards to transportation, both surface and air. Does smog also affect the weather?

It seems that it does. A government report cites a "conspicuous increase" in the number of foggy days per season in smog areas. This is hardly surprising, although perhaps in London the people have tolerated fog so long they don't connect it with air pollution. Adding smog doesn't merely reduce visibility, it also cuts the amount of solar radiation reaching the earth through its dirty canopy. For example, solar radiation reaching Phoenix,

Arizona, on some days late in 1966 was only half the normal amount because of smog.

Among the factors affecting the amount of solar radiation reaching the earth are carbon dioxide, water vapor, and ozone (triatomic oxygen, a pale-bluish gas with a fresh, penetrating odor). Industry and transportation contribute the first two of these, obviously. Not as obviously, smog results in an increase of ozone as well. Studies of the problem in Los Angeles revealed that ozone was present in the ratio of about $\frac{1}{2}$ part per million, some 10 to 20 times higher than elsewhere in the country. Where was this 1,000 tons of ozone coming from? At last it was learned that a photochemical reaction was taking place. Sunlight and smog—an ironic combination—were teaming to produce ozone plus other oxidation products.

Studies in Europe of three affected cities showed that the intensity of solar radiation was lowered by 11 per cent to 36 per cent, the higher figure when the sun's slanting rays in morning or afternoon traversed a longer path through the smog layer. Here was an average reduction of something like one fourth of the heat reaching the ground, a cooling effect that might well be a factor in weather.

Astronomer Donald Menzel, among others, sees the possibility of the past ice ages being caused by volcanism. Volcanoes inject great quantities of dust into the air, and this dust can be the condensation nuclei for precipitation. Interestingly, Menzel points out that rainmaker Schaefer has found minute particles of silicon dioxide in a glacier in Alaska. He estimates that only some 500,000 tons of nuclei material would be needed to make possible great worldwide precipitation. Los Angeles alone, remember, was adding 50,000 tons daily.

CARBON DIOXIDE

Smog adds particles of foreign material to the atmosphere, some of which may serve as condensation nuclei for raindrops or snow. Smog also adds carbon dioxide. In fact, even where there is no smog evident to signalize the dirty work in progress, man is adding carbon dioxide everywhere he is operating engines of practically every kind. Only electric batteries (and fuel cells, of which there are only a handful as yet) add no carbon dioxide. Other electricity is generally produced in the first place by a heat engine, which does contaminate the air.

Carbon dioxide is no stranger to earth's atmosphere, of course. We pointed out that the first man added a bit of the gas to the air around him each time he opened his mouth to exhale. Carbon dioxide is important in the life cycle, and nature has adjusted to it and it to her, during the ages that our ecology has been in operation. Besides being a vital factor to life, carbon dioxide is also vital to weather.

Our atmosphere acts as a globular greenhouse, letting in the rays of the sun and holding in the reflected heat from earth. Adding carbon dioxide has the effect of creating a better green-house, the gas acting as a kind of one-way heat valve. The carbon dioxide absorbs so little of the extremely short-wave rays coming from the sun that adding more carbon dioxide has little effect on how much radiation reaches the earth. But the carbon dioxide is quite opaque to the long-wave heat radiation sent skyward by earth.

While the breathing of one individual has no noticeable effect on a world of atmosphere, the coming of civilization joined many men in efforts that seem to have at last produced noticeable feedback for the air we breathe. Estimates of the carbon dioxide content of the atmosphere indicate that the growth of agriculture since the middle of the nineteenth century has raised the carbon dioxide content of the atmosphere something like 4 per cent.

Even this increase is minor compared to the contribution of man's fires and combustion engines. In 1940 a scientist compared the content of carbon dioxide then with that known to have existed in 1900. In those four decades the amount of gas present grew from 290 parts per million to about 320 parts per million, an increase of 10 per cent. By 1958 the carbon dioxide had increased to 330 parts per million, or about 14 per cent more than at the turn of the century.

Paralleling the increase of carbon dioxide in the atmosphere is the evidence that the temperature of the earth has increased since the beginning of this century. The increase, however, is only a fraction of a degree Centigrade, and some researchers suggest that even an increase of carbon dioxide content to 600 parts per million in the atmosphere, or double that at the beginning of this century, will boost the temperature only a degree or so.

None of us has directly noticed the increasing temperature but many scientists are concerned over possible changes in climate by increasing carbon dioxide content. It is generally believed that the ice ages were brought on by a change of only some 10 degrees Centigrade. Although there is some disagreement on this score, it is obvious that a carbon dioxide content geared to our consumption of fuel is bound to rise with increasing rapidity. And changes of even a degree in earth's temperature should not be treated as inconsequential. Indeed, two scientists involved in studies of man's effect on weather have said:

Human beings are now carrying out a large scale geo-physical experiment of a kind that could not have happened in the past nor be reproduced in the future. Within a few centuries we are returning to the atmosphere and oceans the concentrated organic carbon stored in the sedimentary rocks over hundreds of millions of years. This experiment, if adequately documented, may yield a far-reaching insight into the processes determining the weather and climate.*

Aircraft and Weather

The development of the supersonic transport was beset with all sorts of complications. The sound barrier, the heat barrier, and even the financial barrier have been cited as reasons for not building it. There is another reason, given less publicity, that concerns us here. Flying at altitudes above 10 miles, these speedy craft will consume fuel at a rate never before achieved in aviation history. The jet is a combustion engine and it spews out an exhaust as copious as the sonic boom is loud. Carbon dioxide and smoke are ejected and as anyone knows who is familiar with the high-altitude contrails of aircraft—a graceful phenomenon

* Roger Revelle and H. E. Suess, *Tellus*, 9, 18.

with us since World War II—water vapor too is dumped into the atmosphere.

Soon-to-be-flying supersonic transports (SST's) will carry a hundred tons or more of fuel, and because the jet engine mixes air with fuel for combustion, almost half again the fuel weight is exhausted as water vapor. An estimated 400 supersonic transports operating on a four-per-day flight schedule will add about 150,000 tons of water vapor to the stratosphere daily! While this account is only about 0.025 per cent of that present naturally in the stratosphere, it is pointed out that if the vapor persisted at that level, rather than settling back to earth, for as long as 10 years, the cumulative effect of this "drop in the bucket" would be one of *doubling* the water vapor content of the upper atmosphere.

Some calculations show that even a fivefold increase of water vapor in the stratosphere would raise the earth's temperature only 1.6 degrees Centigrade, and perhaps the persistence time of 10 years is far too long. However, it is also true that because of the concentration of routes about half the water vapor injected by the SST's will occur in only about 5 per cent of the stratosphere. Locally the increase will be 10 times the average saturation and this may result in some change in cloud cover and precipitation.

SPACE-AGE WEATHER

It was noted that smog has a number of environmental side effects, one of the seemingly minor ones is that of affecting the electric field of the atmosphere. Increasingly we are learning how important such fields are; perhaps they are a factor in precipitation, for example. There are additional ways that man is altering the atmosphere; he is doing this with another kind of pollution called "radioactive fallout."

The atomic age added a new dimension to man's contamination of his environment. The phenomenon of radioactive debris has received much consideration since it began to sift down from bomb explosions, but there is another aspect of nuclear fission of concern to the atmospheric physicist. While most of us are concerned with the particles that descend, the physicist is keeping a weather eye on materials introduced high in the atmosphere which remain in the atmosphere for some time and diffuse over a wide area. If the naturally present traces of elements in the atmosphere are of importance as environmental factors, what of additional amounts that man is injecting with nuclear-bomb bursts high over the earth?

Bombs exploded in the upper atmosphere have added enough of the light metal lithium to "completely overwhelm" the amount present naturally. The twilight emission of lithium at times has been almost entirely from artificially injected lithium.

There are also sodium, potassium, magnesium, calcium, hydrogen, nitric oxide, and other minor constituents in the atmosphere. Man adds to these with bomb explosions and also adds other materials such as strontium, tungsten, and the like. The cessation of above-ground testing of nuclear weapons following the 1961 tests may have been a blessing to world weather, although it is as difficult to prove that there has been an effect as that there has not.

Even without exploding bombs, the space program introduces large amounts of water vapor. It is estimated that one large rocket motor now on the drawing board will inject 0.3 per cent as much water vapor above 100 kilometers as now exists there naturally. Thus a few more than 300 such rockets would double the water vapor content, assuming that diffusion carries the vapor all about the upper reaches of the atmosphere. Before this diffusion takes place there will of course be local conditions of far more than normal amounts of vapor. One survey arrives at the conclusion that to double the amount of water vapor with present rockets would require launching somewhere between 1,000 and 10,000 of them a year. Space planners are not yet this busy on the launch pads but it is foreseeable that the world may one day launch 300 large rockets in a year.

Even with no bombs exploding in the atmosphere, then, it is still possible to contaminate the tenuous gases nature put there in the first place. The result, according to the National Academy of Sciences, is surely some local disturbance of the photochemistry or radiation balance of the upper atmosphere.

We have noted that the electric fields in the atmosphere may be a factor in precipitation. Another indication is that global weather is affected by the interaction of the "solar wind" of charged particles and the earth's magnetic field. Atom bombs bursting in the region of this field have demonstrated their ability to set up new magnetic fields and to alter the existing ones.

Atom bomb tests in 1961 created a new radiation belt about the earth by injecting electrons into the magnetic fields that encircle it. Immediate damage was done to solar cells and electronic equipment aboard orbiting spacecraft which moved through the man-made radiation. Scientists predicted that the belt might remain for from several years to hundreds of years. If the natural radiation belts are an intermediary factor in the transfer of energy from the sun to earth's weather factory, might there be some interaction between man-made belts and nature's energy supply?

There are stories about the man who set out to rid his barn of rats but burned the whole building down in the process, and another man who killed more game by accident than when he set out to hunt in earnest. We are finding ourselves in this same bumbling category with regard to our inadvertent effects on weather. If man can do something about the weather completely by accident, how much more might he do by design?

"It is not strange that such an exuberance of enterprise should cause some individuals to mistake change for progress, and the invasion of the rights of others for national prowess and glory."

—Millard Fillmore

11

The Dangers of Tampering

Is weather changing justified, or should man let well enough alone? There are two schools of thought concerning the things that rainmakers and other weather experimenters are doing and considering doing. It is not difficult to make a case for either side. Hurricanes, for example, do an estimated damage of $250 million a year to property in the United States; it is impossible to put a price tag in dollars on the deaths they cause. Surely if we can save lives and money with cloud seeding or other techniques, this would justify the modification of weather. But suppose some unexpected meteorological side effect results that in the long run causes even more devastating havoc than the suppressed storms would have?

It might well be asked if there are alternatives to the changing of weather. For example, could we improve blind-landing equipment for aircraft to make such a description truly meaningful? Could we relocate agriculture and animal-raising operations where there is an abundance of moisture rather than try to bring the moisture to where these operations are now? Might not builders stay out of areas likely to be flooded during heavy rains, or might not protective dams be built or some sort of diversion of

Boeing Aircraft

Some authorities say that hundreds of high-flying supersonic transports will double the amount of water vapor in the atmosphere in ten years.

natural waters solve the problem? Could adequate warning of approaching storms, coupled with different building techniques and a good evacuation system save much of the loss of life and property caused by hurricanes and other wind storms? Here weather prediction is substituted for weather modification.

Other developments might be called upon in place of weather modification, the National Science Foundation suggests. Man has created microclimates for home, office, vehicles, power lines, and even his agricultural fields. It is reported that the yield of corn in the United States from 1929 to 1962 increased because of technology of seed, fertilization, and cultivation. The crop also became less dependent on variations in the weather. However, it seems inevitable that man will pursue the course he has begun to change weather itself.

The age of scientific weathermaking was preceded very slightly by the nuclear age. From the first blasts of atomic bombs it was

Our space effort also contaminates the upper atmosphere to some extent.

evident that here was not only a terrible direct weapon but also a source of potential unknown dangers. Attempts have been made at the international level to control experiments with nuclear explosions because of the known dangers and the even more dangerous possibilities as yet unknown in detail. Awful as the nuclear bomb is, however, some scientists have suggested that weather modification is potentially a greater force. For example, the use of weather as a weapon of war, with crippling fogs and rains visited on the enemy's troops and parching droughts created to destroy his homeland. A bullet or bomb is faster, but food and water can win a war simply by being withheld.

We already have problems aplenty because of our propensity—or necessity, perhaps—for dumping garbage into water and air. What will be the long-range effects of seeding the atmosphere intentionally with silver iodide or other materials? Man has already adversely affected the atmosphere without even trying; will he make it worse on purpose, or will he succeed in the coming attempts to control weather for the good of mankind?

THE LAG IN CONTROL OF WEATHER MODIFICATION

How does it happen that 20 years have passed since the first generally recognized successful cloud seeding and we still do not have an adequate machinery for controlling and monitoring weather-modification attempts? Some of the difficulty may be traced to the skepticism of much of the scientific community—and of the pertinent government agencies as well—as to the effectiveness of rainmaking and the other modification operations. In spite of the apparent success of weather changers in hundreds of documented projects here and abroad, uncertainty prevailed in scientific circles, government, and among the lay public. While technology flourished, the science, at least that part of it involved with investigating long-range human effects, lagged far behind.

It was a decade after Schaefer's pioneering cloud-seeding flight before President Eisenhower's Advisory Committee on Weather Control published its report. In an appendix, this report suggested a need for more research into the effects weather modification might have on human beings. However, no particular group was charged with such a responsibility and thus no concerted effort was made to attack the problem.

In July, 1958, President Eisenhower approved Public Law

85-510, authorizing and directing the National Science Foundation to initiate and support research and evaluation in the field of weather modification. There was still no agency given the specific task of investigating the human effects of weather modification, and apparently because of the uncertainty of the effectiveness of rainmaking and other techniques, very little was accomplished in this direction.

Only in October, 1963, was a Special Commission on Weather Modification authorized by the National Science Board and appointed the following year. This Commission was asked to examine the physical, biological, legal, social, and political aspects of weather modification and make recommendations for future policies and programs.

On December 20, 1965, the Commission completed its report, from which some information for this chapter is drawn. In general, there are two inherent dangers in weather modification: legal difficulties, and actual harmful effects resulting from changing the weather. The first of these dangers had already manifested itself, as the report pointed out in four conflicts that may result "or have already resulted" from weather modification projects:

1. Research on the techniques of weather modification is likely to encounter conflict with other research programs unless there is a clear agreement as to the time and place of each field experiment. Otherwise, operations in the area may cause contamination and thus run the risk of invalidating the observations elsewhere.

2. Growth of weather-modification operations could make it impossible to carry out carefully controlled experiments. Were farmers in the Great Plains to become generally convinced that cloud seeding could increase rainfall at critical periods or could suppress hail, their activities soon would cover the area so thoroughly that without regulation it would be difficult to run experiments to find out whether or not the operations were in fact effective.

3. A conflict arises where one group stands to benefit from

weather modification and another to lose. As already noted, this may apply both within a single area and between two areas.

4. There is the possibility of conflicts between groups seeking to modify weather for different purposes or for the benefit of different areas. Rather than there being unintended effects upon other groups from one seeding operation there can be direct conflict over the use of a site or atmospheric conditions.

The legal ramifications are broad enough that they will be considered separately in the next chapter. We are concerned here with the actual physical consequences of weather tampering.

THE HUMAN EFFECTS OF WEATHER

The National Science Foundation report, *Weather and Climate Modification,* has this to say in a section entitled "The Human Effects of Weather and Climate Modification."

Like other recent technological advances, weather and climate modification techniques, if fully effective, present humanity with unprecedented opportunity *and grave danger.* [Italics added for emphasis.] So pervasive are the elements of weather in the mind and works of man that an alteration in one of them, even over a small area, may provoke intricate social changes. Some of these changes are obvious but many are difficult to trace and puzzling to measure.

As an example, the benefits of fog dispersal to permit airplane flights are cited. But another and unwanted result of this same operation might be the icing of highways adjacent to the airport, to the harm of surface traffic. Effects then are not always direct, but more often come indirectly through alteration of the hydrological, biological, or ecological systems.

Instead of proceeding in a straight line from weather-modification projects to benefit mankind, results come from the interaction of four interrelated systems: atmospheric circulation, the hydrological cycle, biological ecosystems, and human production. This complex and circuitous route from cause to effect means that in many cases man cannot know just what he is triggering when he attempts large-scale modification of the weather.

Historically, such ignorance of what he is about has not dissuaded man from going ahead with modification projects in other fields. Huge forests and grasslands have been exploited, farmland ruined by shortsighted and economically selfish operations, lakes spoiled perhaps for all time by thoughtless dumping of refuse into them. Even when men *know* an action is harmful, they often continue to pursue the easy course, as in the case of smog pollution. It is hoped that in the field of weather modification more restraint will be used and a more scientific and objective look taken into the future that probably results from certain operations on the atmosphere.

A factor that complicates the problem is the ease with which some cloud-seeding operations are conducted. With a few hundred dollars' worth of dry ice, or silver iodide, experimenters seemed to alter the course of a large hurricane and to introduce periodic heavy rains thousands of miles from the seeding location. Anyone with an airplane or a ground-based generator can cheaply play hob with passing clouds. Dr. Langmuir sincerely believed that for a pittance he had drastically changed the weather of much of the United States. If he was right, and a single silver-iodide generator could accomplish this feat, what is possible using more advanced technology and better seeding agents? This is one of the big problems facing the serious experimenter in weather modification, and also those charged with looking after the public good. For man, in his haste even to do good for his fellow man with weather changes, may take too short a view and do greater harm than what he tries to cure.

BIOLOGICAL IMPLICATIONS OF WEATHER MODIFICATION

There are many obvious possible dangers in tampering with weather, such as creating arid zones downwind of seeded areas, and detrimentally altering the pattern of winds or inducing tornadoes or other damaging storms. Changing the climate might melt icecaps and flood much of the coastal areas. There are other, less obvious dangers even more directly concerned with life.

The report *Weather and Climate Modification* says: ". . .

changes in rainfall or temperature which are of sufficient magnitude to have general usefulness seem likely to be of sufficient magnitude to produce substantial disturbances in natural communities."

The eye of Hurricane Esther (1961) from 20,000 feet. These clouds form the floor of the "eye." The central cloud with a convective structure is the characteristic hub-cloud of a hurricane.

Average annual temperature changes of 3 degrees to 4 degrees Fahrenheit can result in the increase or decrease, or even the appearance or disappearance, of some types of plants and animals, although hardwood forests and grasslands remain relatively unchanged. A change of temperature of 6 to 8 degrees Fahrenheit would result in displacement of many species by others, great population changes, and sometimes the replacement of one major kind of natural community by another.

Of interest is the fact that rainfall is most important during a certain period, a few critical months rather than the whole year. A relatively minor increase of rain could greatly affect population, causing either explosion or extinction.

It should be noted that while increased precipitation in an area can lead to either benefit or harm, decreased precipitation in another area—which might result if the rain-shadow theory (prevention of rain downwind of the area in which rain is artificially produced) is correct—can result in no benefits.

In the natural community of today the picture has changed from precivilized times. Once a species was more or less free to migrate when conditions changed so as not to favor that species. If rain ceased, animals or men trekked off to a wetter region. Today, there are "islands" of wildlife surrounded by humans, a sea of humanity that prevents migration as effectively as a watery sea would. Displaced animals are thus faced with a choice of marching lemminglike out onto the freeways or curling up and dying where they are.

Increasing rain over an area that is capable of growing plant life will increase the production of crops, unless the increase is enough to flood the land or to ruin it for agriculture by washing away the productive soil. In a world where the cry is for food for the increasing billions of humans, more crops would seem at first suggestion an unmixed blessing. Unfortunately the scientists studying the problem feel that the picture is not all bright and uncomplicated.

The natural community includes insects along with man, plants, and animals. Increased rainfall results in a decrease in some insect pests, including the chinchbug, for example, and some cutworms. But on the whole, more rain means more pests to eat up the crops. From time to time it has been pointed out that insects may one day inherit the earth, since they are more stable than animals. It would be ironic if man himself hastened the day with what he conceived as beneficial weather modifications.

Not only insect pests, but organisms that cause disease may also be affected by weather. It is known that disease germs carried by "arthropod" (invertebrates with articulate body and limbs) intermediate hosts are dependent on weather conditions, and perhaps other diseases also fall in this category. These arthropod-carried germs cause disease of a serious kind in man and domesticated animals.

Interestingly, the outbreak of insect pests is thought to be touched off in a particular part of a region by an unusual weather situation. When the insect population builds up sufficiently it begins to spread out in all directions like a wave. It is noted that this phenomenon is similar to the spread of many human diseases, including bubonic plague. While scientists do not foresee an epidemic of plague as a result of weather modification, they point out that such a thing could possibly happen. Bacterial and fungal diseases of crops are also responsive to the weather. Thus plant pathogens (specific causes of disease) would be affected by changes in temperature and moisture.

PSYCHOLOGICAL CONSIDERATIONS

One very real consideration that must be taken into account is the psychological effect of publicized weather modification on the people affected, or who imagine themselves to be affected. Knowing that the government has decided to risk harm to the few for the good of the many might change the mental processes of the few—and perhaps the many as well. There might be a balancing benefit in the form of a scapegoat for those down on the weather. Here would be a handy whipping boy for every flood or drought that came along.

One aspect of weather modification not obvious at a glance is the spiritual and aesthetic effects that result. The National Science Foundation report on weather modification suggests that the battle of man against the elements—the extremes of heat and cold and driving wind—is a source of deep satisfaction to the human soul. The savage blizzard and the frightening and awesome lightning bolt remind us dramatically of our physical puniness alongside nature's elemental forces. Assuming that the weather changers are one day able to pull the teeth of the lightning storm and to hush the raging winds, what effect will this staid and stable atmosphere have on a human spirit that evolved in a much more turbulent environment?

What Should We Do Now?

The National Science Foundation Commission reports the following conclusions and recommendations:

1. Living things are adapted to the weather that actually prevails, and any change in that weather will generally be deleterious to them.

2. The largest credit item for weather modification is likely to be an increase in primary production of the drier parts of the land surface through improvements in rainfall. Even the ability to control seasonal distribution of rainfall would lead to more efficient farming operations. Realization of the potential increase in production would depend upon being able to modify the rainfall without major pest outbreaks and extinction and disruption of natural communities. It is not certain that this would be possible.

3. The largest weather-modification debit item is likely to spring from the decreased stability of communities, which would manifest itself in an increase in pests, weeds, and pathogens. The identity of the species involved in these disruptions cannot be predicted, nor can their cost.

4. For the present, weather and climate modification should be restricted to local and small-scale operations.

5. Larger-scale operations, such as an attempt to increase the rainfall of any substantial part of this country, should not be undertaken, from a biological point of view, in the present state of knowledge.

6. All weather-modification experiments of a scale large enough to have important biological consequences, such as those currently envisioned for the Upper Colorado Basin, should be preceded and accompanied by careful ecological monitoring and

computer simulation studies. Manipulating the weather to obtain a net benefit will demand much better understanding of the interactions of weather, climate, and organisms than is now available.

7. Adequate understanding of the interrelationship of weather, climate, and ecology will demand a very expensive long-term research program. Present resources of ecologically trained investigators are inadequate to cope with these problems.

LOOKING AHEAD

Two approaches to assessing the effects of weather modification are suggested. One is to assume a particular type of modification, the dispersal of fog, for instance, and then to estimate the consequences to the human community. A second and more long-range method would be to inquire at what points our social system would be sensitive to weather changes, and then to estimate which changes would be more desirable, without considering if such changes are presently feasible. Obviously the first approach, empirical in nature, is the easier of the two. What work has been done in assessing possible benefits and dangers has been accomplished in this way. It has been suggested that the second approach be used to supplement this.

The electronic computer, heart of new weather-prediction systems, can also be used to predict the results of man's intervention in the weather. By feeding into the computer the changes planned by the weather modifiers, scientists can learn what other effects, besides those sought, might result. This simulation technique will be used to assure that catastrophes caused by unwise weather modification occur in the computer, and only in the computer. For example, the National Center for Atmospheric Research is directing computer studies of the results of melting the ice in the polar regions. The computer is being asked to show resulting changes in weather and climate over the world for the next several hundred years.

It is becoming painfully apparent that the weather changer has forged mankind a key to the Pandora's box of weather, a box that is proving not always to be filled with pure blessings. The long-range results of cloud seeding or other weather-modification schemes are not always apparent at the outset; a trouble pushed down at Spot A on the globe may perversely pop up twice as large at Spot B—and trigger a gunshot from a resident of B at one of A. If the pilot of a light plane armed with a couple of pounds of dry ice can touch off a lawsuit by irate neighbors, large-scale weather changing has the potential of international friction stemming from upsetting weather patterns. Weather changers would do well to look carefully and perhaps count to ten before leaping at clouds with silver linings.

"He maketh his sun to rise on the evil and on the good, and sendeth rain on the just and on the unjust."

—MATTHEW 5:45

12

Weather Modification and the Law

IF I make it rain on my ranch and you suffer a drought some distance downwind of me, can you sue me for stealing your precipitation? Or for flooding out your property? If one group seeds clouds to prevent hail, can another group collect damages claiming that rainfall was reduced? If a state engages in weather modification for the benefit of its people, can an individual enjoin the state on the grounds that he is being injured? If Operator O seeds clouds over State A which drift over State B and cause floods that damage property there, should the courts of State A or B, or the Federal government have jurisdiction in the suit?

These are samples of the legal problems stemming from man's deliberate tampering with nature's weather. A decade ago *Fortune* forecast "high legal winds" as one result of cloud seeding and other such projects; there have indeed been court battles over alleged misuse of dry ice and silver iodide. The question of to whom the weather belongs has not yet been satisfactorily answered, and it may be some time before it is. One bothersome aspect of the problem is the fact that not much can be done until specific cases arise, because of lack of precedent. Yet if we wait until the damage is done it may be too late to help very much in the courts.

The Legal History of Weather

There is presently no body of law, either common or statutory, that concerns itself directly with modification of the weather. The courts must therefore look to existing common law for hints and guidelines to the rights and duties of those who would modify the weather, and those affected by such modification. A promising avenue toward this goal is a survey of property rights to find what title, if any, the ownership of land conveys to the owner with respect to the atmosphere above it. For example, water rights are part of property rights, both with respect to ground water and to bodies of water. Internationally there is the "three-mile limit" off the coast.

Byzantine Emperor Justinian codified the Roman law in the sixth century and the Institute of Justinian stated that all things are the property of someone or of no one. The jurist R. J. Pothier wrote that the first of mankind possessed in common all those things God had given to the human race, and described this community as a "negative community," in that nothing belonged any more to one of them than to another. Gradually, however, the idea of property rights as private with individuals came into being, perhaps because of the basic "laws" of human nature. Early common law conferred rights of use, and these rights developed into a system of actual ownership of various objects.

The well-known idea that possession is nine points of the law harks back to these early common-law property rights. Ownership was based on occupancy, and occupancy implied control or dominance of the occupied territory, plus the intention to use it. Obviously then, there was no ownership of areas that could not be occupied. No one owned an unscalable mountain, for instance, or a sea in the days before boats were invented or stumbled onto. And no one owned the sky before the airplane soared into that domain. Even today the air is still listed as common property, although many laws governing its use have been made. For example, aircraft are forbidden to fly over certain areas, and producers of aerial pollutants are in some cases forbidden to dump more than a certain percentage of such wastes into the atmosphere.

In addition to the air, other "common property" includes the sea (except for the three-mile limit already mentioned), running water, and wild animals. Blackstone* phrased such common property this way:

Fire, light, air, and water. . . . A man can have no absolute property in these, as he may in the earth and land; since they are of a vague and fugitive nature, and therefore can admit only of a precarious and qualified ownership, which lasts so long as they are in actual use, but no longer.

The millowner, for example, could use the stream to drive his wheel, but had no further claim over the water downstream. Surely the clouds above are of a vague and fugitive nature, hard to get a grip on even when one can climb into their realm. However, Accursius (Accorso), an Italian jurist, is generally credited with introducing the law known as *ad coelum,* or "to the sky" doctrine. In general this states that he who owns the land owns also the sky above it. It is believed, however, that Accursius had in mind the rights of owners of burial plots to have such land free from overhanging buildings. Thus the dead might be said to have rights in both directions; down to perdition and up to heaven.

Careful examination of the basis for the *ad coelum* doctrine is described as its downfall, and to some the doctrine of Accursius is an accursed piece of commentary. A precise translation of the complete Latin phrase that Accursius wrote in the margin of his commentary is that the property includes the air "up to" the *coelum,* and not the *coelum* or sky itself. Other Latin scholars describe this right as extending only a little above the highest treetops and buildings. Today, with the Empire State Building

* *Commentaries,* sec. 395.

and others, rather than the few stories of early Roman times, the untangling of the doctrine is a bit more difficult.

From a strict legal viewpoint, *ad coelum* is not the law and never was the law. It was in actuality only a figurative phrase expressing full and complete ownership of land itself and the right to whatever superjacent airspace was necessary and convenient to enjoyment of that land. However, in recent times property owners have sold airspace rights above their holdings; for example, the sale of the right to build a freeway over certain private property.

Among the newer theories cited for airspace rights are the following:

1. The "zone theory." Airspace is divided into two zone layers and the landowner owns absolutely the lower layer but not the upper one. This is owned only to the extent necessary for him to own the airspace in order to use the land below. (Isn't rain *necessary* for farming?)

2. The theory adopted by the Uniform State Law for Aeronautics. The surface owner has unlimited ownership of the upper airspace subject only to the public's privilege of flight. It would permit the landowner to own the clouds, but raises the question whether the landowner could prevent others from seeding the clouds above his ground under the guise of privileged flight.

3. The theory which limits the landowner's ownership to only that portion of the atmosphere he actually uses. Under this theory the only way the landowner could claim ownership of the clouds would be to use them.

4. The "nuisance theory." This is the more generally accepted theory. It recognizes the ownership of the upper airspace and grants the remedy for nuisance when actual interference occurs. The landowner under this theory has only reasonable use of the clouds and is liable if his use creates a nuisance to others.

Now we come to the water vapor residing in the air, and what sort of property rights are involved here. A parallel seems to be the common-property status of animals *ferae naturae,* or wild animals. As long as these animals are in their natural wild state they belong to no one. But as soon as someone tames or domesticates them, or even captures them for a zoo, they become private property. The first person who "occupies" them owns them.

U.S. Department of the Interior

A high school student seeds vapor-laden air with a basket of dry ice at Old Faithful Geyser. This caused moderately heavy snowfall half-a-mile downwind.

A landowner is protected by a number of natural rights. These include principally riparian rights; the right to the support of land; and the right to use land for any reasonable purpose. The landowner is also entitled to use rainfall, and now we are getting to the crux of the problem of rainmaking law. The property owner uses the precipitation only after it falls. While it is still in its vaporous state, he maintains no control over it, and thus cannot claim ownership. Rather, he could not until quite recently.

Riparian rights are based on the fact that the owner's property is washed by flowing water. The key here is natural flow of the water, and it is not legal to tamper with the water upstream of the landowner by damming it, diverting it, or otherwise changing the course of nature. Riparian rights endow *use* of the water, not the water itself.

Here are two laws that seem applicable to weather modification: riparian rights and the right to natural diffusion of the atmosphere. A man may use the water and air coursing along and over his property, but may divert or pollute neither of them. He may also insist that no one else do these things to his detriment. And here is the parallel. The clouds have been described as "rivers in the sky," and the phrase is becoming increasingly popular as weather-modification projects increase. Yet clouds by their nature are not as constant as most land-based rivers and are instead "vague and fugitive" in their nature, as Blackstone pointed out.

To further cloud the issue—or muddy the waters—of weather-modification legalistics is another kind of water right that has superseded the riparian law in much of the American West. This is the prior appropriation right, and came largely from the operation of the placer miners in California. This doctrine considers water as belonging to the people in common, but permits preferential rights to someone who can show an intent to use the water for a beneficial purpose. This includes building a canal and using *all* the water, as for a factory or other industry.

Those studying the prior-rights doctrine do not feel that it applies to rainmaking since the rainmaker would not have diverted the clouds from their natural course, nor would he have any control over the water in them after it reached the ground as rain. It would seem, however, if the rainmaker seeded clouds with the intent of irrigating a wheat ranch, for example, such use would constitute control of the rainfall after it landed.

Another body of existing law covers the "percolating" waters, the waters under the ground. Common law conveys this water use exclusively to the owner of the land containing it. However, in the United States most courts follow another doctrine, called the reasonable-user rule. This restricts removal of percolating waters for some useful purpose on the land from within which the water is taken. Because of some similarity of the percolating underground waters to the "rivers in the sky," these rights are described as tempting by those studying application of existing law to weather modification.

Thus far, attempts to contrive weather-modification law have been on the basis of analogy to existing law, such as water law or oil and gas law. However, depending too much on this crutch is as bad as attempting to start from scratch and create new laws applying only to weather modification.

Modern Legislation

The Standard Legislative Review has described rainmaking as "a natural for governmental regulations." Basic to this not surprising judgment are the several powers granted by the Constitution to Congress, in particular the commerce clause and that having to do with interstate commerce. A number of cases have been cited as clear indication that weather modification does indeed affect interstate commerce and that Congress has the "unquestionable power" to control it.

Public Law 83-256 (67 Stat. 559), August 13, 1953, created the Advisory Committee on Weather Control to study and evaluate public and private experiments in weather modification. Public Law 84-664 (70 Stat. 509), July 9, 1956, extended the life of the Advisory Committee on Weather Control for two years to June 30, 1958. Public Law 85-510 (72 Stat. 353), July 12, 1958, authorized and directed the National Science Foundation to initiate and support a program of study, research, and evaluation in weather modification. As we saw in the first chapter, there is other legislation now under consideration which will greatly increase government support of weather modification and also apply controls to it.

STATE LAWS ON WEATHER MODIFICATION

As yet no specific Federal regulations have been set up regarding weather modification, although some states have passed legislation in this field. For example:

Arizona licenses weather control projects, and requires the filing of descriptive reports.

California licenses all persons engaged in weather modification and requires a notice of intent prior to any project.

Colorado claims the right to all moisture suspended in the atmosphere over it, and the prior right to increase precipitation of that moisture by artificial means. The division of natural resources of the state licenses "qualified applicants" for weather control of cloud-modification projects.

Connecticut has established a weather-control board concerned with the theory and development of weather modification and control, utilization of weather modification and control for various purposes, and also the protection of life and property during such activities.

Florida licenses weather modifiers, and requires proof of financial responsibility and a record of all operations.

Hawaii has empowered its board of land and natural resources to investigate the possibility and feasibility of inducing rain by artificial or other means.

Idaho requires weather modifiers to register and keep a record of their activities.

Louisiana claims a sovereign right to use the moisture contained in the clouds and atmosphere within state boundaries for the best interests of its people. It also licenses those engaging in weather modification.

Maryland has prohibited any form of weather modification for a two-year period ending in 1967.

Massachusetts issues licenses to qualified applicants for weather-modification projects. Required is a publication of intent by the licensee and a public hearing.

Nebraska law provides permission for weather control and regulates persons active in weather-modification projects. The state has also created weather-control districts within its boundaries, although a previous act of this nature was declared an unconstitutional delegation of power by the State legislature.

Nevada empowers its director of the state's department of conservation and natural resources to establish advisory com-

U.S. Department of Commerce, Weather Bureau

Who is to blame if this sort of damage follows the attempts of a cloud seeder?

mittees for weather-modification matters, and also to license persons engaged in such work.

New Hampshire has authorized any department or agency of the state to engage in experimentation in weather modification, with the approval of the Governor and council.

New Mexico in 1965 required licensing of persons attempting to control the weather. It was from Socorro, New Mexico, that

Dr. Langmuir claimed to have caused the heavy periodic rains in 1949 and 1950.

North Dakota not only requires the registration and licensing of those engaged in weather modification, but also authorizes the counties within the state to levy taxes to pay for the services of rainmakers. This was 1965 legislation.

Oregon requires licenses, and also proof of financial responsibility.

Pennsylvania in 1965 passed an act granting each county the authority to prohibit weather modification it considered detrimental to the county's welfare.

South Dakota claims its sovereign right to use for the best interests of its residents the moisture contained in the clouds and atmosphere within the state boundaries. It has a weather-control commission that licenses those engaged in weather modification.

Utah requires those who intend to engage in weather-modification attempts to notify the state School of Mines and Mineral Industries of the University of Utah before each attempt, and also to submit a report of each such operation.

Washington has established a weather-modification board, requires licensing, and grants a permit for an operation after a hearing by the board. It also requires proof of financial responsibility.

Wisconsin requires weather-modification people to register each operation with the public service commission and file a report with the commission after the operation.

Wyoming has claimed its sovereign right to use for its residents and best interests the moisture contained in the clouds and atmosphere within its state boundaries. It has also created a weather-modification board and licenses those engaged in this work.

Maine reported that weather modification was of no significance within its boundaries because it initially possessed such fine weather! However, there are twenty-two states now having statutes dealing with at least some aspects of weather modification. Only two of these states list specific requirements to be met by would-be weather makers as indicating their competence in the field. Several states have followed the lead of all nations in claiming absolute sovereignty of airspace above their territory. Two states limit weather-modification activities that may affect other states, and one state has also barred all weather modification for two years. Several states exempt themselves and their instrumentalities from liability for weather modification by private persons.

Six states do not require any licensing. Arizona requires licensing unless the rainmaking is attempted over the operator's own land. Those selling rainmaking equipment must also be licensed and also report all sales. Of the sixteen states requiring licenses, only Wyoming requires that the applicant must be a professional engineer. Washington stipulates that the applicant be a member of the American Meteorological Society, or be qualified to become a member.

For ninety license applications, only one was denied and one revoked. Licensing fees range from $10 in North Dakota to $200 in Nebraska. Emergency licenses may be granted for such purposes as fog suppression and control of fires.

Kentucky is liable on a negligence basis up to $10,000. No state relieves private persons from liability. Oregon requires financial responsibility in the amount of $100,000 for property injury and $100,000 for personal injury.

RAINMAKING LAWSUITS

Since the first witch doctors began trying to make it rain or stop raining they have been paying for the consequences—often in the early days with their lives or at least their jobs. The weather as nature doles it out cannot please everyone, and so when puny man begins to intervene the rain is bound even more to fall on the just and the unjust alike. And when you flood my property or parch my cornfield with your artificial wringing of the clouds nearby I am going to do one of two things. I may throw rocks at you and your airplane, or even shoot bullets with the intent to hit the infernal target; or I may take legal action. The miracle of modern rainmaking is not so much that it works, but that so few actual lawsuits have developed.

As of this writing, there have been eight lawsuits stemming

from weather modification in the United States. All of these
involved cloud seeding. Of the eight, one was abandoned before
a court decision was reached. Two others have not yet been
prosecuted. Of the remaining five, one in Texas was decided in
favor of those seeking an injunction against the weather modifiers; the others went in favor of the rainmakers. Let's look at
these cases in detail.

Slutsky et al. v. the State of New York

In 1950 New York City experienced a terrible drought, and
water for domestic purposes was critically short. In desperation
the city fathers engaged the services of Dr. Wallace E. Howell, an
authority on artificial cloud seeding, whom we have mentioned earlier. Whether or not Howell's rainmaking operations
were responsible, the precipitation feeding the reservoirs increased and yielded an additional two-week supply for the city's
water drinkers. However, not everyone applauded this operation.
Among those who felt injured was a resort owner in Ulster
County, the watershed area being seeded, and he brought suit
against the city fathers, seeking to have them stopped entirely
from conducting the operation. His objection is understandable,
since resortgoers are not particularly happy to have their vaca-
tions spoiled by rain.

The suit claimed that the proposed rainmaking experiments
would result in inundations, swell the streams of the Catskill
Mountains watershed inordinately, and cause considerable damage to the owners of property along such streams. These owners
were protected by riparian water laws. It was also pointed out
that rain, or even the threat of rain, would be harmful to the
resort business. The court had this to say in denying the petition
for injunction:

> The court must balance the conflicting interests between a remote
> possibility of inconvenience to plaintiff's resort and its guests with the
> problem of maintaining and supplying the inhabitants of the city of
> New York and surrounding areas, with a population of about 10 million
> inhabitants, with an adequate supply of pure and wholesome water.

The relief which the plaintiffs ask is opposed to the general welfare and public good; and the dangers which plaintiffs apprehend are purely speculative. This court will not protect a possible private injury at the expense of a positive public advantage.

This decision was based simply on the judgment that the plaintiffs had no vested property rights in the clouds or the moisture therein. Writers have stated that this decision appears based not on rules about property rights and water rights, but on principles of equity and public-policy ideas concerning the general welfare and the public good. Further it is suggested that the decision might have been different had the plaintiffs asked monetary relief, rather than seeking to bar New York City from attempting to increase its water supply.

Another party not wanting the rain Howell was credited with producing was the Palisades Amusement Park in New Jersey, which reportedly offered him double pay to *stop* the rain!

Township of Ayr v. Fulk

In 1964 Dr. Howell figured in a second lawsuit. A group of fruit growers in Pennsylvania, West Virginia, and Maryland hired him to modify the weather in their behalf. Hail sometimes destroys crops of fruit to the tune of millions of dollars, and the Blue Ridge Weather Modification Association was formed to suppress hail by seeding the offending clouds. Unfortunately for the fruit growers, neighboring truck farmers in Ayr Township of Fulton County, Pennsylvania, felt that Dr. Howell was all too successful and was in fact stealing rain from them. They claimed that his seeding operations resulted in a drought. In reprisal they stole the silver-iodide generators and also cut down hundreds of the fruit trees of their "enemies." Finally, Ayr Township passed an ordinance that made it illegal to engage in weather-modification activities:

Section 1: No person or persons shall install, construct, erect, operate, or maintain any equipment, machinery, or device within the said township designed to, or intended to, or which has a tendency to eliminate, regulate, or interfere with the normal rainfall or precipitation, or engage in rainmaking, cloud seeding, hail dispersement, hail chasing, or maintain or operate equipment or device known as ground-based generators used in connection with rainmaking, cloud seeding, hail dispersement or hail chasing whereby smoke or vapors are discharged into the atmosphere for the purpose of or which tend to affect the normal precipitation or rainfall.

A fine of from $100 to $300 would be imposed for each day of violation of the ordinance.

Later, Mr. Fulk, a cloud seeder, set up a silver-iodide generator and was convicted of violating the ordinance by a Justice of the Peace. He appealed the case to a higher court, claiming that he was not attempting to modify the weather in Ayr County, but only in nearby Maryland. He hoped that expert testimony would prove that this activity could have had no effect at all on Ayr Township and no harmful effect to anybody outside the Township.

Pennsylvania Natural Weather Association v. Blue Ridge Weather Modification Association et al.

In another Pennsylvania suit, filed against the Blue Ridge Weather Modification Association, the Pennsylvania Natural Weather Association brought charges. Among these were the release of dangerous chemicals into the air, interference with the rights of landowners to receive rain, hail, snow, and fog on their land in their undisturbed character, and so on.

Samples v. Irving P. Krick, Inc.

In 1953 Irving P. Krick, Inc., seeded clouds over the North Canadian River watershed for Oklahoma City. While this operation was going on a cloudburst and flood occurred near El Reno, Oklahoma. The landowner filed suit, charging negligence on the part of Krick. However a jury found the defendant not guilty of negligence, although how a jury of nonscientific people could be expected to judge whether or not a cloud-seeding operation was conducted negligently, since even scientists cannot agree on the process, is open to serious question.

Auvil Orchard Co., Inc., et al. v.
Weather Modification, Inc., et al.

Another suit was filed in Chelan County, Washington, in 1956. Auvil Orchard Co., Inc., sued Weather Modification, Inc., for flash floods that occurred on their property during cloud seeding over adjacent territory to prevent hail. In this case the court granted a temporary order banning further hail-suppression activities. However, after testimony by expert witnesses, the court refused to make the ban permanent.

Adams et al. v. The State of California et al.

A more serious suit was filed after a damaging flood of the Feather River in California in December, 1955. The Pacific Gas & Electric Company had for some time been operating ground-based generators to seed the clouds to increase precipitation for hydroelectric power production. Lives were lost and great property damage was incurred. Property owners sued the State of California. This case was not settled until April, 1964, at which time the court found that Lake Almanor, where the seeding had been done, had successfully impounded all precipitation feeding into it, and thus that cloud seeding could not be charged with contributing the water that flooded the Feather River.

Southwest Weather Research, Inc., v. Jim Duncan et al.

In Texas a group of farmers hired Southwest Weather Research, Inc., to conduct operations for the suppression of hail. Neighboring ranchers claimed that such modification of the weather would rob them of rain, and sought a permanent injunction against the operators. The trial court temporarily enjoined the rainmakers' activity in the vicinity of the ranchlands supposedly robbed of moisture. The appellate court affirmed the decision, but modified the injunction to prohibit weather modification only in the area directly over the plaintiff's land. The purpose of the injunction, in the words of the court, was to "preserve the status quo until complicated scientific problems and attendant legal questions can be fully considered and a final judgment rendered determining the rights of all parties involved."

In the Southwest Research restraining suit, the hiring farmers lived in and around Fort Stockton, east of Jeff Davis County in Texas. The trial court found that the weather modifiers were

flying airplanes over appellees' lands, and expelling a foreign substance into the clouds above appellees' lands in such a manner that there was a change in the content of the clouds, causing them to be dissipated and scattered, with the result that the clouds over plaintiffs' lands were prevented from following their natural and usual course of developing rain upon and over and near plaintiffs' lands, thereby resulting in retarded rainfall upon plaintiffs' properties.

Expert witnesses disagreed in their testimony. Two stated positively that seeding clouds could not deplete or destroy the rain potential of them if they might have produced rain otherwise. Another witness, however, stated that overseeding of potential clouds could diminish or destroy their rainmaking power. Vincent Schaefer, surely an authority, was also quoted:

On the other hand, if through accident or design a storm is overseeded, the effect can be to form so many ice crystals that they disperse the moisture in the freezing zone and thus destroy the basic conditions for precipitation. This is the process involved in hail dispersion.

Among the witnesses called were ranchers in the area, some who had lived there since before the turn of the century and claimed to have become skilled in evaluating clouds for their rain potential. These witnesses testified that on many occasions when potential rainclouds or thunderheads were overhead the hail-suppressing airplanes flew through the clouds and that in ten to twenty minutes the clouds were destroyed or dissipated. One witness called the shapes produced by seeding like a "nightmare." Another said he would "remember to his dying day" what the seeding planes did to the rain clouds.

WHO WILL CONTROL THE WEATHER CONTROLLERS?

A legislator has wisely pointed out that it is far safer for experimenters to conduct rainmaking and other weather-modification projects in remote areas where there is only wildlife. Lions and goats, he says, are not very litigious. Realistically, however, weather modification affects humans, including the irate and uneducated as well as the legitimately concerned.

Because we are learning that there are no islands as far as weather is concerned, there are beginnings of reciprocal agreements between and among states. This is particularly understandable in light of the fact that weather modification has crossed not only state lines but those of countries as well. Members of the Canadian House of Commons have accused their own government and the State of New York of a conspiracy leading to heavy rains in upper Quebec. This occurred in spite of the fact that the rainmakers supposedly responsible gave assurances that no such projects were in progress in the area, and the records of the Weather Bureau showed no increase in precipitation. Yet doctors reported that health was affected adversely in the area in question, and their bills were sent to the local government for payment. Quebec canceled all rainmaking experiments in 1965 as a result of the public clamor against them. Attempts at controlling the weather have resulted in not only threats but gunfire directed at seeding aircraft. A National Science Foundation report points out that attempts at major weather-pattern alterations may come to be a *casus belli* in international affairs.

It is obvious that one of the major problems of weather modification is the legal problem. It is often difficult to unravel ownership of land and the air space above it; the question of who owns weather is much knottier. Land stands still, and so does the sky above it, but weather is transient. State boundaries and even national boundaries cannot contain weather. A new "shot heard round the world" may be that of a hail gun or nuclear blast intended to divert the path of a hurricane.

Experiments must be allowed to continue, if progress is to be made. But there must be safeguards at the same time to guard against weather catastrophes of man's own making. Since weather is not fenced in by political lines, and conditions vary widely from one end of the country to the other, control over those who would in turn control the weather poses a legalistic problem worthy of a Solomon.

While the states have taken the initiative, many of them suggest that Federal control is indicated and necessary if the interests of the general public and those specially concerned with weather are to be protected against the abuses of the self-seeking and the incompetent. Because of this, the legal climate of the future is of great importance to the weather modifier, and weather law seems destined to be an important branch of the judicial system.

"Measures in the arctic may control the weather in temperate regions, or measures in one temperate region critically affect another, one-quarter around the globe. All this will merge each nation's affairs with those of every other, more thoroughly than the threat of a nuclear or any other war may already have done."

— JOHN VON NEUMANN

13

Weather Changing Around the World

WEATHER modification is not the special province of the United States. Men were seeking to change the weather long before Columbus discovered America, although perhaps the American Indians had been as successful with their rain dances and other exhortations to the gods of weather as had rainmakers in the Old World.

If we are bound together internationally, our common problems help in the binding, and of these weather is perhaps the commonest. In every language men talk about the weather, and men of most languages seem to be trying to do something about it. At a time when shortages of water and food already are of some concern in various parts of the world, the global importance of weather modification is obvious and many countries are involved in projects of varying scope and size. Not surprisingly, Russia leads the world in weather-modification effort. Some authorities estimate that the Soviet Union devotes from two to three times more effort and money to this work than the United States does. Published scientific material in this field is 34 per cent Russian, with the United States a close second at 29 per cent. The remainder is divided among some twenty other nations.

The National Academy of Sciences–National Science Foundation report on weather modification includes the following comments on Russian work:

The delegation of the U.S. Weather Bureau which visited the Soviet Union in May 1964, returning a similar visit to the United States by Soviet scientists earlier that year, was particularly impressed by the broad scope of the Soviet program and the large resources of manpower and funds that were being concentrated on weather modification and related activities. Although actual work is undertaken in a number of institutes located in various parts of the Soviet Union, and includes activities in both the Arctic and Antarctic, the Soviet activities appear to be well integrated into a national program and guided toward the achievement of objectives directly related to the economic and social needs of the country.

Russian work began in the late 1940's, and has included all the types of modification research conducted in America, plus work with acoustical techniques for precipitation and studies of warming the Arctic region artificially. The year 1962 was an "all-cloud" year for Russian scientists. Claims of a saving of 10 million rubles in hail damage in 1964 and an increase of 10 per cent in precipitation by seeding frontal clouds have been made, so it is understandable that the Russians have assigned a higher priority to weather modification than the United States has.

Among the other nations active in weather-modification operations or research are the following:

Argentina: Work includes a five-year program in experimental hail prevention using silver iodide. Indicated a 70 per cent reduction in hail damage when cold fronts are seeded; but 100 per cent *increase* in hail damage on other seeded days.

Australia: Began in 1947 with cloud seeding for precipitation. Under auspices of the Commonwealth Scientific and Industrial

Research Organization. Many years of cloud seeding, without positive conclusions being reached. Recent concentration on natural nucleation, and formation of ice in clouds.

Canada: Cloud seeding for rain began in 1948. Hail-abatement studies and experiments conducted since 1956 in the Alberta hail belt. Also, controversial rainmaking experiments in Ottawa and Quebec areas more recently.

Communist China: A twelve-year plan was begun in 1956 in meteorology. Includes cloud seeding with dry ice or salt, quick-lime, water, salt solution; warm cloud work using salt solution and flaked ice and glacier blackening, using coal dust and burned grass or wood.

France: Cloud seeding for rainmaking and hail suppression in the mountains since 1950. Also engaged in fog suppression at airports.

Germany: Research into cloud physics, including atmospheric electricity and coalescence phenomena, hail prevention, and fog dissipation.

Great Britain: Research programs including electrical charge separation, coalescence, and ice-crystal growth.

India: Cloud-seeding experiments, including use of salt as nuclei.

Israel: Studies of correlation of rainfall and presence of nuclei, plus wind direction.

Italy: Cloud-seeding experiments since 1950. Use of small rockets in hail abatement in grape orchards on a commercial basis. Also research on the electrification of atmospheric dust as it affects the formation of water droplets.

Japan: Research in cloud physics, emphasizing ice crystals. Seeding experiments begun in 1951 have led to reported increases of 10 per cent to 20 per cent in summer precipitation.

Kenya: Use of Italian antihail rockets on a tea-growing estate from 1962 to 1964 demonstrated significant reductions in hail damage.

Korea: Cloud-seeding experiments planned for the area around Seoul.

Mexico: Cloud-seeding experiments begun in 1953.

Environmental Science Services Administration

A supercooled cumulus cloud "explodes" after being seeded with silver iodide in 1963 experiments. The photographs were taken (1) immediately after seeding, (2) nine minutes after seeding, (3) nineteen minutes after seeding, and (4) thirty-eight minutes after seeding. Dr. Langmuir claimed aerial seeding of this sort swerved a hurricane that later hit and severely damaged Savannah, Georgia.

Panama: Wind-suppression schemes in 1959.

South Africa: Cloud seeding begun in 1947.

Sweden: C. G. Rossby was interested in dusting snow fields to speed melting in spring. His death halted plans. Professor Tor Bergeron interested in climatic-change studies.

Switzerland: Began in 1950. Conducting laboratory research in growth of hailstones.

Tunisia: Fog suppression at airports, using liquid propane.

Individual nations have been able to gain knowledge in space and nuclear energy unilaterally. With weather, however, it is more necessary to cooperate. Although atmosphere is shared by all nations, basic information essential to successful large-scale weather modification appears to be unobtainable unless all na-

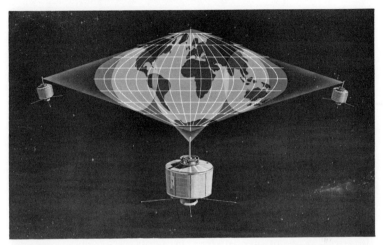

Hughes Aircraft Company

How satellites can keep track of the world's weather is shown by these three "synchronous" satellites, each stationed one-third of the way around the earth.

tions cooperate in gathering and making available data from their atmosphere.

In his classic article, "Can We Survive," scientist John von Neumann discussed the global implications of weather and climate control. Setting a price tag on altering climate at something like the cost of establishing the railroads in the United States, he went on to show how much more significant large-scale climate control would be.

"There is no need to detail what such things would mean to agriculture or, indeed, to all phases of human, animal, and plant ecology," von Neumann said. "What power over our environment, over all nature, is implied!"

All this, he stated, would merge each nation's affairs with those of every other, more thoroughly than the threat of a nuclear or any other war may already have done.

It has been pointed out that for each class of weather modification—fog suppression, rainmaking, hail suppression, hurricane alteration, and large-scale climatic modification—there is some probability of success. That probability is high for fog suppression and ranges downward to close to zero for changing climate over a large area. Fortunately the international ramifications of each of these weather phenomena are in inverse order to their probability of achievement. Climatic change, with greatest global implications, is least likely to be achieved. Fog suppression is a practical actuality but has least chance of causing international problems. However, the fact that the atmosphere belongs to the earth as a whole makes it inevitable that juggling the weather in the United States may some day affect the weather in some other country.

In addition to individual efforts in the field of weather modification by nations, there is also some international effort toward an orderly prosecution of such experiments.

The World Meteorological Organization (WMO) was formed in 1951, replacing an earlier organization. In that same year weather modification was placed on the list of subjects to be studied. By 1955 WMO prepared a report entitled *Artificial Control of Clouds and Hydrometeors,* a rather cautious examination of cloud-seeding experiments to date.

On December 20, 1961, the General Assembly of the United Nations passed Resolution 1721, on the peaceful uses of outer space. This resolution pointed to the "greater knowledge of basic physical forces affecting climate and the possibility of large-scale weather modification" as a primary goal of research and development in atmospheric science and technology. Orbiting weather satellites were beginning to demonstrate their ability to give meteorologists, and indeed the general public, a picture of global weather undreamed of only a few years earlier.

The General Assembly resolution also asked that the World Meteorological Organization, together with UNESCO and other specialized agencies and organizations, prepare a report on ways and means of achieving better weather forecasts and advancing the state of the art of weather modification through space satellites. A key statement in the subsequent WMO report referred to conscious and unconscious modification of weather and climate as a problem requiring international planning and cooperation:

Ultimately mankind may well have the power to influence weather and even climate on a large scale. However, it is imperative that the consequences of any large-scale interference with the atmosphere be accurately evaluated in advance.

The general theme of the report was that understanding the modification of weather on the large scale required complete knowledge of the global circulation of weather. At the request of the WMO Advisory Committee, Professor L. Krastanov of Bulgaria prepared a paper entitled, "Possibilities for an International Cooperation in Research Work Done in the Field of Cloud and Precipitation Physics." Krastanov stated that research thus far in weather modification has shown how very complex the problems are, and also indicated the need for help from disciplines other than meteorology alone. He called for a coordination of scientific effort at the national and international level, and a similar merging of technologies to implement operations.

To implement this coordination, Krastanov offered a six-point program, which is summarized below:

1. A general program for new research in the field of cloud and precipitation physics, with the joint efforts of the World Meteorological Organization, International Union of Geodesy and Geophysics, and International Council of Scientific Unions. Such a program would define more precisely the directions of the research and serve as a part of the over-all program for the atmospheric science.

2. Different countries were invited to participate with their own national programs, drawn up in accordance with their abilities.

3. Within the WMO, a coordination center would be created, composed of experts on cloud and precipitation physics. Every country having a national program would participate in the center with a representative of its own whose expenses would be paid by the country.

4. In every country, a national scientific (coordinational)

committee for cloud and precipitation physics would be created to work out and approve the national program on the basis of the general program and to coordinate the scientific research within the country. Each country decides for itself to which of her state institutions the national committee should be attached.

5. Each national committee would keep in touch with the WMO Secretariat as regards the exchange of national reports on the research work done and the exchange of scientific information among the participating countries.

6. The national committee could conclude bilateral or multilateral agreements for joint scientific work and for an exchange of specialists and scientific information.

As a result of the Krastanov paper, the WMO Commission for Aerology created a working group on cloud physics including Krastanov, V. T. Nihandrov of Russia, Professor Louis J. Battan of the University of Arizona, and experts from Japan and India. An international conference on cloud physics, under the auspices of the International Union of Geodesy and Geophysics tentatively will be held in 1968. The United Nations Economic and Social Council (ECOSOC), whose responsibility it is to improve the economic status of less-developed countries, held a conference in 1963, which explored the possibility of artificial rainfall. A report issued after this conference stated:

We have been impressed by the progress already achieved in the field [of weather modification and control], but equally by the gaps in the basic knowledge of the atmosphere, and particularly of the upper atmosphere, which will need to be made good before weather modification could become a practical possibility. Nevertheless, in the long term, weather modification might hold out dramatic possibilities as a future means of influencing environmental conditions in a manner favorable to agricultural production, and development of research in this field should, in our opinion, be kept under constant review.

The IUGG's Committee on Atmospheric Sciences held its initial meeting in 1965, and later issued a report which included the following comments:

A prerequisite for the scientific exploration of large-scale climate modification is the ability to assess the probable consequence of conscious intervention in natural weather processes. Global dynamic modeling techniques, to which reference has already been made, are a powerful tool with which to assess these consequences and to design scientifically meaningful experiments to be conducted in the atmosphere. At the moment, the use of mathematical models for this purpose is seriously hampered by precisely the obstacles this program is intended to remove.

NASA

Engineer tears photo from facsimile recorder receiving pictures of global weather transmitted by Tiros satellite.

Any contribution to an understanding of the scientific possibilities and limitations of large-scale climate modification would be of great importance. Moreover, it is highly desirable that such studies proceed as an international cooperative effort.

The Committee set as a goal a fully developed atmospheric research program by the end of 1967.

WORLD WEATHER WATCH

As D. S. Davies, Secretary-General for the World Meteorological Organization, points out, ". . . for the main part the meteorologist's laboratory is the atmosphere itself. He cannot control his experiments and even to observe events as nature produces them, over an area of the Earth's surface sufficiently large to permit useful studies and deductions, raises many difficulties."

Davies also points out that TOS, the Tiros Operational Satellite, has made it possible to detect and follow any major storm all over the world. WMO suggested that satellites, and other developments including the electronic computer, be incorporated into a single coherent world weather service which it has named "World Weather Watch" (WWW).

The basic aim of WWW is to provide meteorological data needed by every country in the world. To do this, three steps are involved: a global observational system (GOS), a global data-processing system (GDPS), and a global telecommunication system (GTS).

The mainstay of the global observational system is the orbiting satellite, since it can "see" at a glance what is happening weatherwise. But GOS also includes land stations, fixed ocean stations, increased use of merchant ships, new balloon-reporting methods, and reports from civil aircraft.

To handle the global data-processing WMO foresees three world meteorological centers, each of which is already actually in partial operation. These centers are in Melbourne, Australia; Moscow; and Washington, D.C. Broadly the responsibilities of the centers are the reception and transmission of weather data on a global scale; preparation and dissemination of weather analyses and predictions on a global and/or hemispheric scale; processing and dissemination of data for climatological and research studies on a global scale; storage of data in a form convenient for subsequent retrieval for climatological and research purposes; provision of training facilities; and conducting basic and applied research on large-scale programs.

Supplementing the world centers will be from twenty to thirty regional and national centers. The final organizational unit is the regional telecommunications hub. These hubs will exchange data between centers.

The objectives of WWW are as follows:

To develop a deeper understanding of the global circulations of the atmosphere and the associated system of climates.

U.S. Department of the Interior

What looks like a jet engine on this Air Force plane is really an instrument pod used in Bureau of Reclamation weather-modification tests.

To place weather forecasting on a firmer scientific basis.

To develop techniques for predictions on extended time scales, and to provide knowledge needed to improve weather forecasts of small space-scales and time-span.

To explore the extent to which weather and climate may be modified through artificial means.

By 1966 training seminars had been held in Moscow and in Tokyo.

INTERNATIONAL WEATHER MODIFICATION LAWS

The Special Commission on Weather Modification of the National Science Foundation in December, 1965, suggested that America go on record concerning weather modification:

The Commission recommends the early enunciation of a national policy embodying two main points: (1) that it is the purpose of the United States, with normal and due regard to its own basic interests, to pursue its efforts in weather and climate modification for peaceful ends and for the constructive improvement of conditions of human life throughout the world; and (2) that the United States, recognizing the interests and concerns of other countries, welcomes and solicits their cooperation, directly and through international arrangements, for the achievement of that objective.

The question of the legal issues involved was also brought up in 1965 by attorney Edward A. Morris in the *Bulletin of the American Meteorological Society*.

The international situation should also be given attention. An attempt should be made to achieve an international agreement on large-scale control. It will undoubtedly be difficult to reach such an agreement, since no one may know exactly what it is we are trying to regulate. However, agreement should be easier and concessions more readily made by a nation which does not know who will be first to achieve the scientific breakthrough than by a nation which finds that it is first, and it then is the only nation to possess, by reason of knowledge or geography, the power to change the climate of other countries.

Harlan Cleveland, former Assistant Secretary of State for International Organization, has stated: "We won't want other nations modifying our weather, and so we will certainly have to accept some restraints on our freedom to modify theirs."

The U.S. Weather Bureau amplified this thought.

As of the present time there are no international agreements or conventions dealing with weather modification activities. But as the scale of weather modification activities becomes larger and as their pace quickens, we may expect the appearance of international agreements

and conventions that will provide a framework for international cooperation, that will require a nation engaged in weather modification
activities to consult with neighboring nations that might be affected,
and that may eventually establish some form of international ramifications. These agreements and conventions are for the future. But when
they do appear, they will materially affect how the Federal Government conducts and supports weather modification activities.

U.S. Department of the Interior

Large radar antennas of the Nike-Ajax anti-missile system are used to
track wind flow and to monitor precipitation during weather-modification studies.

For many reasons, both common sense and legalistic, the
weather makers are bound to consider their neighbors around
the world as they go about the work of making deserts bloom as
the rose and frozen regions melt for habitation and agriculture.
We may feel called upon to project national boundaries into the
sky, but nature won't see them. Weather and climate are global
affairs and he who juggles them had best take the long look
first.

14

Looking Ahead

PREDICTING the future of weather modification is an even more difficult task than predicting the weather. Captain Orville was premature in his estimate of the coming of very accurate quantitative weather prediction, and the wisest heads in weather modification are being cagier. No one is betting money on rainmaking or other facets of the business within "X" years, even on a "percentage of probability" basis. We'll not be dialing weather for the neighborhood, or the city, for that matter, within a decade. But practical weather modification as a general thing seems to lie ahead somewhere over the horizon.

It has been pointed out that the atomic age is in its third decade without widespread peacetime power applications. Space exploration too takes time, and may well require the energies of a generation before it lives up to its bright promise. Both these fields have profited from the expenditure of billions of dollars and millions of man-hours of time, compared with the modest effort invested in weather modification. So we must not hope for a bargain in miracles from the rainmakers. With all these cautious qualifications, however, the timetable tentatively set offers a pleasant surprise.

In January, 1967, as this book was being completed, Secretary Udall suggested that by 1972 Americans might be increasing precipitation in the United States. To achieve this goal he outlined fifty experimental projects, plus twenty actual pilot

U.S. Department of the Interior

University of Wyoming personnel prepare a radar-tracking balloon for launching during Bureau of Reclamation weather-modification tests.

rainmaking projects, costing a total of perhaps $100 million in the next eight years. The results, if successful, would include application of seeding techniques to increase orographic rainfall over parts of Colorado and Wyoming by 1972; operations in the southern Sierras a year later; and increased precipitation in the central mountain region and areas of the Northwest, the north Plains, and the southern Plains-Gulf region by 1975.

Pointing to the fact that about 47.5 billion acre-feet of water flows across the country in the "rivers in the sky" each year, the Secretary's report suggests tapping an additional 2 per cent of this supply. This modest increase through artificial seeding would increase America's rainfall by a whopping trillion gallons a day! Best of all, this would not represent "robbing Peter to pay Paul," but would be a net gain benefiting all.

Such plans will make use of the many techniques discussed in earlier chapters, and perhaps others as well. Research continues on many fronts. For example, in Arizona the Rev. Kieran McCarty, a Franciscan priest at San Xavier Mission, is studying old records in an effort to tell physicists at the University of Arizona's Atmospheric Physics Institute just what caused the sudden drought that created the Sonoran Desert in northwestern Mexico and southern Arizona. This happened only seventy-five years ago, and was caused either by overgrazing by huge herds introduced by Texas cattle interests or by some natural climatic change as yet not understood.

Another suggestion that man has intervened to his own dis-advantage in weather came recently from Vincent Schaefer. Smog, in the form of lead particles from auto exhausts, is the culprit, if Schaefer's theorizing is correct. These particles may cause large numbers of ice crystals to form, thus preventing growth of crystals large enough to result in precipitation. Per-haps the antipollution forces will have to link arms with the rainmakers for the common good.

Another form of transportation may become a factor in future weather modification. It has been suggested that the railroads, with their extensive rights-of-way, are ideally situated for rain-making experiments and operations. Perhaps the locomotive of the future will be a double-duty piece of equipment, hauling freight and passengers, and at the same time seeding the sky with silver iodide.

There is always the chance that serendipity will come to the fore again as it did for Schaefer in 1946 and that a deceptively simple and highly effective technique will supplant current methods. Whatever the case, it is no longer true that nobody does anything about the weather. For better or for worse, man is changing it, just as he set out to many centuries ago.

Index